Josephus Collett

Spelling book

Josephus Collett

Spelling book

ISBN/EAN: 9783743311633

Manufactured in Europe, USA, Canada, Australia, Japa

Cover: Foto ©Paul-Georg Meister /pixelio.de

Manufactured and distributed by brebook publishing software (www.brebook.com)

Josephus Collett

Spelling book

PREFACE.

The experiment of dispensing entirely with the spelling book as a text-book in schools has not met with the success that its advocates anticipated, and the return to a word-book of some kind is becoming general. The book demanded by the times, however, is not merely a compilation of words arranged in columns to be memorized by the pupil, but a series of language exercises teaching the origin, structure, sound, and meaning of words, presented in an attractive and suggestive manner.

The plan of this *Spelling Book* is inductive; beginning with a careful study of the sounds of the words, it proceeds to the correct methods of writing their forms, and closes with exercises pertaining to the process of word-building and the sources of the words themselves. Root-words and words in every-day use are largely employed, and frequent lessons in grouped objects, synonyms, and dictation exercises are introduced.

Throughout the book reference is constantly had to the meaning of the words, and efforts have been made to expose the common errors in spelling, pronunciation, and the use of words.

Copyright, 1891, by
JOSEPHUS COLLETT.

INTRODUCTION.

THE English Alphabet consists of twenty-six letters, five of which (*a, e, i, o,* and *u*) are called *vowels,* and the others *consonants.* *W* and *y,* usually consonants, are sometimes vowels, and their vowel sounds are the same as *u* and *i.*

A *Vowel* is a letter which can be perfectly sounded without the aid of any other letter.

A *Consonant* is an articulate sound, in utterance usually combined and sounded with a vowel.

A *Diphthong* is the union of two vowels in one sound.

The vowels, and some of the consonants, have several sounds; in this book these sounds are indicated by *diacriticals,* as follows:—

KEY TO PRONUNCIATION.
TABLE OF VOCALS.
Long Sounds.

ā,	as in	āte.	ē,	as in	ēve.
â,	"	eâre.	ẽ,	"	ẽrr.
ä,	"	ärm.	ī,	"	īçe.
ȧ,	"	lȧst.	ō,	"	ōde.
a̤,	"	a̤ll.	ū,	"	tūne.

ōō, as in fōōl.

INTRODUCTION.

Short Sounds.

ă, as in ăm.
ĕ, " ĕlm.
ĭ, " ĭn.
ŏ, as in ŏdd.
ŭ, " ŭp.
o͝o, " lo͝ok.

Diphthongs.

oi, as in oil. | ou, as in out.

TABLE OF SUBVOCALS.

b, as in bĭb.
d, " dĭd.
g, " ḡīḡ.
j, " jŭḡ.
n, " nīne.
m, " māim.
ng, " hăng.
l, as in lŭll.
v, as in vălve.
th, " thĭs.
z, " zĭne.
z, " ăzure.
r, " râre.
w, " wē.
y, " yĕt.

TABLE OF ASPIRATES.

f, as in fīfe.
h, " hĭm.
k, " cāke.
p, " pīpe.
s, " sāme.
t, as in tärt.
sh, " shē.
ch, " chăt.
th, " thĭck.
wh, " whȳ.

INTRODUCTION. v

TABLE OF SUBSTITUTES.

ạ,	for ŏ,	as in	whạt.	y̆,	for ĭ,	as in	my̆th.
ĉ,	" â,	"	thêre.	ҽ,	" k,	"	ҽăn.
ẹ,	" ā,	"	fẹint.	ç,	" s,	"	çīte.
ï,	" ē,	"	polïçe.	çh,	" sh,	"	çhāiṣe.
ī,	" ẽ,	"	sīr.	ҽh,	" k,	"	ҽhāos.
ȯ,	" ŭ,	"	sȯn.	g̣,	" j,	"	g̣ĕm.
o̱,	" ōō,	"	to̱.	ṉ,	" ng,	"	iṉk.
o̤,	" ŏŏ,	"	wo̤lf.	ṣ,	" z,	"	ăṣ.
ô,	" a̤,	"	fôrk.	s,	" sh,	"	sụre.
õ,	" ẽ,	"	wõrk.	x̱,	" g̱z,	"	ĕx̱ăet.
ụ,	" ŏŏ,	"	fụll.	gh,	" f,	"	läugh.
û,	" ẽ,	"	bûrn.	ph,	" f,	"	phlŏx.
ṳ,	" ōō,	"	rṳde.	qu,	" k,	"	pïque.
ȳ,	" ī,	"	flȳ.	qu,	" kw,	"	quit.

In this book the *u* in *qu* is canceled when the *q* is sounded like *k;* also the *h* in *ch* when the sound is that of *k*.

For the *names* and *offices* of *diacritical marks*, and those of other signs used in writing and printing, see Lessons 148, 149.

Part I. of this book, pages 9–64, furnishes numerous illustrations of the above sounds, incorporated with the main text.

Silent letters have been canceled by a line drawn diagonally across the letter.

THE ALPHABET.

A	a	N	n
B	b	O	o
C	c	P	p
D	d	Q	q
E	e	R	r
F	f	S	s
G	g	T	t
H	h	U	u
I	i	V	v
J	j	W	w
K	k	X	x
L	l	Y	y
M	m	Z	z

SCRIPT ALPHABET.

CAPITAL LETTERS.

A B C D E F G H I

J K L M N O P Q R

S T U V W X Y Z

LOWER-CASE LETTERS.

a b c d e f g h i

j k l m n o p q r

s t u v w x y z

THE MANUAL ALPHABET.

GOOD   BAD

1 2 3 4 5 6 7 8 9 10

Learn this alphabet. You can then converse with the deaf. It will aid you in spelling. Turn the palm of the hand toward the person addressed.

SPELLING-BOOK.

PART I.—ORTHOEPY.

In this department are given the sounds of the vowels, interspersed with script exercises, words of opposite meanings, grouped objects, and other exercises.

Lesson 1.

Short sound of a, marked ă.

ăt	băt	hăd	făn	băḡ
ăn	măt	măd	păn	hăḡ
ăm	păt	păd	lăp	lăḡ

The lad ran. She had a fan.

Lesson 2.

Short sound of e, marked ĕ.

bĕt	bĕd	fĕn	mĕt	wĕb
ḡĕt	fĕd	tĕn	sĕt	wĕd
pĕt	lĕd	dĕn	lĕt	wĕt

He fed the hen. Did she get wet?

Lesson 3.

Short sound of i, marked ĭ.

lĭp	bĭd	fĭḡ	hĭt	fĭn
sĭp	dĭd	dĭḡ	fĭt	pĭn
hĭp	lĭd	bĭḡ	pĭt	jĭḡ
dĭp	rĭd	wĭḡ	bĭt	sĭn

Lesson 4.

Short sound of o, marked ŏ.

cŏt	bŏḡ	pŏp	pŏt	cŏn
dŏt	fŏḡ	mŏp	pŏd	sŏb
ḡŏt	jŏḡ	sŏp	nŏd	sŏd
nŏt	lŏḡ	tŏp	rŏd	rŏb

The fox hid in his den.

Lesson 5.

Short sound of u, marked ŭ.

rŭt	bŭn	bŭd	rŭb	hŭḡ
cŭt	dŭn	ḡŭn	tŭb	lŭḡ
hŭt	jŭt	pŭn	dŭḡ	rŭḡ
bŭt	fŭn	mŭd	rŭm	tŭḡ

SPELLER. 11

Lesson 6.
THINGS THAT HAVE LIFE.

băt	măn	năḡ	ŏx	hŏḡ
eăt	lăd	hĕn	fŏx	bŭḡ
răt	răm	pĭḡ	dŏḡ	pŭp
erăb	stăḡ	fĭsh	frŏḡ	dŭçk

The dog bit the rat.

Lesson 7.
Long sound of a, marked ā.

hātę	eāmę	rāçę	ḡāy̨	fāi̯l
mātę	fāmę	māçę	māy̨	jāi̯l
lātę	dāmę	lāçę	sāy̨	rāi̯l
rātę	lāmę	fāçę	dāy̨	nāi̯l

Lesson 8.
Long sound of e, marked ē.

mē	fēę	sēęk	pēą	rēąm
wē	trēę	lēęr	nēąt	mēąl
yē	fēęl	jēęr	bēąm	mēąd
shē	rēęl	mēęk	sēąt	bēąd

Lesson 9.

Long sound of **i**, marked ī.

bind	lïng	fīre	hīve	wīng
fīnd	mīne	mīre	dīve	bīle
kīnd	dīne	tīre	kīte	bīte
mīnd	fīne	wīre	rīde	wīde

Lesson 10.

Long sound of **o**, marked ō.

ōld	bōat	lōbe	hōne	bōde
hōld	gōad	lōpe	bōne	bōre
gōld	lōad	rōpe	bōlt	tōld
cōld	tōad	hōpe	tōne	fōld

Lesson 11.

Long sound of **u**, marked ū.

ūse	tūbe	mūte	hūge	tūne
cūe	cūre	lūte	dūke	lūre
hūe	dūre	cūbe	dūpe	Jūne
sūe	pūre	dūne	dūe	fūme

The duke tuned the lute.

SPELLER.

ADDITIONAL MONOSYLLABLES.

Short vowel sounds.

Lesson 12.

eăb	bĕġ	bĭb	bŏx	eŭd
eăn	lĕġ	dĭn	eŏb	hŭb
făġ	ġĕm	ġĭġ	eŏġ	hŭm
năb	kĕġ	ġĭn	fŏb	jŭġ
răn	kĕn	hĭd	fŏp	mŭġ
săġ	Bĕn	kĭt	hŏd	nŭn

Lesson 13.

săp	nĕt	mĭd	hŏt	nŭt
tăn	pĕġ	rĭb	jŏb	pŭġ
tăp	sĕx	rĭm	lŏp	sŭn
tăx	lĕft	sĭx	lŏt	mŭm
văn	tĕll̸	tĭn	mŏb	tŭn
wăġ	tĕnt	wĭn	ġŏnℊ	fŭzz̸

Lesson 14.

băc̸k	fĕlt	dĭsh	eŏst	dŭsk
bănd	lĕnd	kĭc̸k	lŏft	dŭst
eămp	pĕst	lĭmp	lŏss̸	hŭmp
dăsh	rĕnt	lĭvℯ̸	rŏmp	lŭc̸k
păc̸k	sĕnd	rĭsk	sŏc̸k	mŭsh
sănd	wĕnt	wĭsh	tŏss̸	mŭst

INDIANA STATE SERIES.

ADDITIONAL MONOSYLLABLES.

Long vowel sounds.

Lesson 15.

fāy	bēef	īçe	dōg	mūle
hāy	rēef	nīçe	wōe	pūle
clāy	hēed	rīçe	flōe	lūke
prāy	wēed	bīde	dōle	flūke
stāy	lēek	hīde	jōke	jūte
trāy	erēek	sīde	mōle	flūte

Lesson 16.

gāme	ēar	fīfe	cōal	mŏst
nāme	fēar	līfe	fōal	hōst
sāme	gēar	wīfe	lōan	clūe
fāde	tēar	dīke	mōan	cūte
wāde	smēar	līke	cōax	flūme
shāde	spēar	strīke	hōax	spūme

Lesson 17.

rāid	bēak	nīng	shōw	snōre
pāid	pēak	pīng	snōw	smōke
māin	hēat	vīng	stōw	spōke
stāin	pēat	shīng	mōre	fūse
trāil	ēase	spīng	lōre	lūng
snāil	grēase	whīng	stōre	jūice

Lesson 18.

REVIEW OF SOUNDS.

From the sounds already learned, require the pupils to mark the following words correctly, canceling the silent letters:

apt	lent	bill	lode	null
tag	bee	hind	lock	pump
babe	belt	hint	oft	glue

Lesson 19.

Sound of the diphthongs **oi** or **oy**, and **ou** or **ow**.

boy	oil	how	pound	fowl
coy	boil	prow	bound	howl
toy	toil	town	sound	cowl

Lesson 20.

Italian sound of **a** as in *arm*, marked ä.

ärg	eär	tärt	pärk	spär
ärt	tär	eärt	bärk	stär
ärk	jär	därt	härk	seär
ärm	␣mär	lärd	bärn	färm

His bark was on the sea.

Lesson 21.

Broad sound of **a**, marked ạ; **o**, marked ô, has the same sound.

balḷ	paw̸	draw̸	ôrb	côrn
caḷḷ	haw̸	flạw̸	cork	bôrn
falḷ	jaw̸	waḷk	fôrk	hôrn
paḷḷ	lạw̸	taḷk	fôrm	lôrd

Lesson 22.

In words of two or more syllables, one syllable receives the chief stress of voice, called the *accent*. The accent is denoted by a mark (′) at the end of the accented syllable; thus, pā′per.

Long sounds of **a**, marked ā, and **e**, marked ē.

bā′bel	fā′tal	dē′çent	nē′ḡro
bā′by	mā′zy	dē′mon	pē′dal
lā′bel	nā′bob	hē′ro	rē′al

Lesson 23.

NAMES OF BIRDS.

owl	lärk	ḡulḷ	quāịl	ḡrouse̸
jāy̸	hawk	w̸rĕn	fīnch	rŏb′in
dȯve̸	crōw̸	crāne̸	snīpe̸	thrŭsh

The owl hoots in the dark.

November 23. Inadi.

2
3
4
5
6
7
8
9
10
11
12
13
14

1,1 1) 5 8 5 7 9,00 (5,3 1,3 4

333

377

333

149

111

380

333

470

2 4 5) 5 3 1, 3 7 4 (4 12 8

496

353

248

1054

16

Lesson 24.

THE WORDS WE USE.

The following words make one third of our common language, written and spoken; and the first ten, one fourth. They appear here in the order of their precedence:

the	Ī	yo̸ṳ	bē	the̸y
ănd	thăt	ā	fôr	shăll̸
ŏf	ĭn	ĭs̤	hăve̸	ăs̤
tọ	ĭt	nŏt	bŭt	hē

Lesson 25.

Long sounds of i and o, marked ī and ō.

bī'as	fī'at	bŏn'y	ō'ver
bī'bl e̸	fī'nal	bō'nus	ō'men
dī'et	ī'çy	tō'per	lō'cal

Holy Bible! book divine!

Lesson 26.

THINGS THAT SHOULD BE SEEN IN A SCHOOL-ROOM

măp	bĕll̸	slāte̸	g̊lōbe̸	pā'per
pĕn	dĕsk	chärt	chạl̸k	rụl'er
ĭṉk	bŏŏk	elŏ¢k	sēạts	pĕn'çil

P. S. B.—2.

Lesson 27.

REVIEW OF PREVIOUS LESSONS.

Require the pupil to write these words with proper accents:

start	caper	tiger	ground
fault	table	pilot	grope
paint	venal	pony	plume

Lesson 28.

Long sound of u, marked ū.

bū'ġlę,	fū'ry	ęom mūnę'	re pūtę'
tū'lĭp	lū'çid	re ṣūmę'	de pūtę'
dū'el	tū'mult	as sūmę'	ęom mūtę'

Lesson 29.

FAMILIAR OBJECTS.

lămp	stōōl	lounġę	ęrā'dlę
vāsę	brōōm	bŏt'tlę	pĭtch'er
ęärd	housę	dĭsh'eṣ	bĕd'stĕạd

Rest not! life is sweeping by:
Go and dare before you die.

SPELLER. 19

ADDITIONAL MONOSYLLABLES.

Lesson 30.

With diphthongs, ä, ạ, and ô.

eoin	joy	lout	eount	vow
join	eloy	pout	fount	brow
ḡroin	soil	flout	hound	plow
nciṣǿ	spoil	shout	houṣǿ	elown
poiṣǿ	joint	snout	mouṣǿ	drown

Lesson 31.
With ä.

bärb	därn	äre	däṉt	härsh
ḡärb	bärk	märl	ḡäṉt	pärch
bärd	märk	härp	häṉt	stärch
härt	spärk	bäth	jäṉt	färçǿ
mȧrt	stärk	läth	täṉt	spärsǿ

Lesson 32.
With ạ and ô.

ạẉǿ	hạlt	wạrn	drạẉl	seôrn
eạẉ	mạlt	wạrp	serạẉl	thôrn
mạẉ	pạẉn	lạṉd	fôrm	tôrch
rạẉ	yạẉn	wạrm	sôrt	ḡôrsǿ
elạẉ	bạld	frạṉd	snôrt	ḡôrḡǿ
erạẉ	wạrd	swạrm	môrn	stôrk

INDIANA STATE SERIES.

ADDITIONAL DISSYLLABLES.

Long vowel sounds accented.

Lesson 33.

bā'sin	lē'ġal	ġī'ant	bō'rax	dū'eal
fā'vor	ġē'nus	mī'nus	nō'blę	jū'lep
mā'sǫn	pē'nal	pī'ǫus	pō'lar	mū'eus
rā'zor	dē'tail	rī'val	sō'ber	pū'pil
wā'ver	sē'quel	tī'tlę	tō'tal	tū'nie

Lesson 34.

bāng'fu̯l	bēę'tlę	plī'ant	pōk'er	fūt'ūrę
eām'brie	mērę'ly	prī'vatę	stō'ry	plū'ral
ġāi'ly	bēak'er	elī'matę	spōk'ęn	stū'pid
rāi'ment	wēą'ry	sçī'ençę	mōlt'ęn	nūi'sançę
sāint'ly	trēą'sǫn	pīę'bald	hōst'ess	sūit'or
trāi'tor	prē'çept	milę'aġę	prō'çęęds	dūkę'dom

Lesson 35.

a bātę'	se vērę'	a bīdę'	mo rōsę'	a būsę'
re māin'	re çēdę'	're mīnd'	pa trōl'	re fūsę'
ob tāin'	ap pēal'	at tīrę'	re pōrt'	as tūtę'
pōr trāy'	re liēf'	pro vīdę'	sup pōsę'	per fūmę'
per suādę'	su prēmę'	re quīrę'	pro vōkę'	pol lūtę'
pro elāim'	a piēçę'	per spīrę'	pōst pōnę'	pur sūit'

Lesson 36.

Short sound of a and e, marked ă and ĕ.

ăb'bĕy   ĕăm'el   fĕr'ry   lĕt'ter
băn'ish   săt'in   fĕt'ter   mĕm'ber
băn'ner   făn'cy   kĕn'nel   mĕn'tal
ĕăb'in   lăd'der   fĕs'tal   pĕp'per

Lesson 37.

The o in *wolf*, the oo in *book*, and the u in *put*, have the same sound, which is shorter in quantity than the oo in *moon*.

put   push   hook   wolf   look
pull   bush   rook   could   took
full   puss   cook   should   shook

The puss could look at the cook.

Lesson 38.

ARTICLES OF FOOD.

hăm   cāke   tärts   chēese
ĕggs   vēal   tōast   bā'con
pīes   pōrk   brĕad   mŭt'ton

Bread is the staff of life.

Lesson 39.

Short sound of i and o.

mĭm′ic	bĭt′ter	ŏf′fer	ĕŏf′feẹ́
ĭn′land	çĭn′der	ŏf′fîçẹ́	ċŏf′fin
ĭn′sĕet	çĭt′y	rŏçk′et	ĕŏm′et
sĭm′plẹ́	crĭçk′et	bŏd′y	ĕŏt′tọ́n

Lesson 40.

DICTATION EXERCISES.

A *mimic* is one who imitates. An *inland* town. The *cricket* is an *insect*. The dead *body* was placed in the *coffin*. He had an *office* in the *city*. *Coffee* grows in warm climates. It was a *bitter* cold day. A *comet* was seen in the sky.

Lesson 41.

ARTICLES OF CLOTHING.

eăp	rōbẹ́	sŏçks	mĭtt́s	ḡlŏvẹ́s̩
hăt	hoŏd	boōts	seärf	băsqụ̈ẹ́
eōạt	săçk	shọẹ́s̩	drĕss̸	bŏn′net
eăpẹ́	ḡown	elōạk	shạẏ′l	măn′tlẹ́

There are other words pronounced like some of the above: cōtẹ́, a small house; săc, a bag for a liquid; băsk, to lie in warmth; and măn′tẹ́l, a shelf above a fire-place.

Lesson 42.

Short sound of u.

ŭn'der	bŭt'ler	fŭn'nel	hŭṉ'ḡer
ŭsh'er	₵ŭm'ber	ḡŭl'let	lŭm'ber
bŭf'fet	₵ŭt'ter	ḡŭt'ter	mŭs'ket
bŭnt'ing	dŭl'çet	hŭn'dred	sŭf'fer

Lesson 43.

Short Italian sound of a, marked à.

påst	ḡràss	bås'kct	a màss'
màss	chànt	₵àsk'et	a vàst'
làst	ḡràft	màs'ter	re pàst'
màst	chànç₵	dàn'çer	en chànt'

This is a medium sound between the ä in *father* and the ă in *fat*, and its mastery should be insisted upon by the teacher.

Lesson 44.

WORDS OF OPPOSITE MEANINGS.

fär	nē₵r	bμ́ȳ	sĕll̸
făt	lē₵n	ḡīv₵	tāk₵
săd	ḡlăd	băd	ḡŏod
hig̸h	lōw̸	härd	sŏft
ŭp	down	sĭ₵k	wĕll̸
nō	yĕs	lärḡ₵	sma̤ll̸

Lesson 45.

Sound of **a** like short ŏ, marked a̤; and **a** as in *air*, marked â.

wa̤d	swa̤n	qua̤sh	flâr𝑒	snâr𝑒
wa̤ş	wa̤sp	wa̤tch	blâr𝑒	seâr𝑒
wa̤nd	wha̤t	eâr𝑒	shâr𝑒	squâr𝑒
wa̤st	squa̤t	dâr𝑒	spâr𝑒	prây𝑒r

Lesson 46.

EXERCISES ON THE ABOVE LESSON.

The *swan* is a graceful bird. A *wand* is a rod. The *wad was* taken from the gun. The *wasp* has a sting. Take *care*, and *spare* no pains. *Quash* means to crush; in law, to make void. *Prayer* is the act of praying. *Watch* and wait.

Lesson 47.

WORDS OF OPPOSITE MEANINGS.

pūr𝑒	foul	sour	swē𝑒t
lŏst	found	dīm	brīght
därk	light	wēa̤k	strŏng
dŭll	shärp	fīn𝑒	eōa̤rs𝑒

Art is long, and Time is fleeting.

SPELLER. 25

ADDITIONAL DISSYLLABLES.

Short vowel sounds.

Lesson 48.

ăb'sent	dĕs'pot	dĭf'fer	dŏl'lar
băl'lot	fĕl'lōw̸	dĭm'pl̸e	bŭb'bl̸e
căn'çel	lĕḡ'at̸e	dĭn'ner	bŭt'ter
făm'ish	tĕm'per	eŏm'mȧ	pŭd'dl̸e
tăb'let	bĭḡ'ot	dŏḡ'mȧ	pŭz'zl̸e
ĕl'bōw̸	çĭv'ĭl	bŏr'rōw̸	sŭl'len

Lesson 49.

drăḡ'on	dĕr'rĭ¢k	ḡlĭm'mer	flŏr'id
flăḡ'on	tĕxt'īl̸e	shĭṉ'ḡl̸e	eŭd'ġel
ḡrăv'el	pĕn'sĭv̸e	swĭn'dl̸e	sŭl'try
plăn'et	mĕs'saḡ̸e	fŏr'aḡ̸e	sŭm'mit
trăv'el	drĭz'zl̸e	fŏr'est	eŭl'prit
dĕn'tist	dwĭn'dl̸e	dŏ¢k'et	jŭs'tĭç̸e

Lesson 50.

flăn'nel	fĕn'çing	frĭe'tion	prŏf'fer
ḡrăm'mar	shĕl'ter	prĭḡ'ḡish	flŭt'ter
plăt'ter	trĕm'bl̸e	skĭt'tish	ḡrŭm'bl̸e
seăn'dal	shĕp'h̸erd	eŏb'bler	shŭd'der
shăl'lōw̸	drĭb'blet	hŏs'tīl̸e	trŭn'dl̸e
plĕn'ty	flĭp'pant	prŏd'uet	stŭb'born

ADDITIONAL WORDS.

Lesson 51.

Sounds of o͝o, ọ, ụ, and o͞o.

wo͝od	wọu̸l̸d	bo͞ot	*bro͞od
wo͝ol	bụl'let	¢o͞ol	dro͞op
sto͝od	pụl'ley	ho͞of	ḡlo͞om
ḡo͝od'nes̸s̸	pụl'let	lo͞op	spo͞on
bọ'ṣom	pụd'ding	po͞or	tro͞op

Lesson 52.

Sound of ȧ.

¢ȧsk	mȧsk	¢rȧft	pȧs'tor
fȧst	dȧft	shȧft	pȧst'ūre̸
ḡȧsp	pȧnt	drȧft	de mȧnd'
rȧft	¢lȧsp	flȧsk	en hȧnçe̸'
tȧsk	ḡrȧsp	lȧnçe̸	en trȧnçe̸'

Lesson 53.

Sounds of â and ạ.

lâi̸r	swe̸âr	wạn	wạf'fle̸
mâre̸	châr'y	swạp	wạr'rant
wâre̸ṣ	pâr'ent	squạd	stạl'wart
lâi̸rd	de ¢lâre̸'	squạsh	quạd'rant
bâi̸rn	¢om pâre̸'	quạr'ry	squạn'der

Lesson 54.

Sounds of e and i before r, marked ẽ and ĩ.

ġẽrm	spẽrm	bĩrd	çĩr'eus
tẽrm	stẽrn	ġĩrl	fĩr'kin
vẽrb	elẽrk	fĩrm	vĩrt'ṳe̸

Lesson 55.

ERRORS TO BE AVOIDED.

In Lesson 25, do not pronounce *bias* bī'us, *diet* dī'ut, *omen* ō'mun, nor *local* lō'kl. Lesson 26, *chalk* is pronounced *chawk*, not *chock*. Avoid the sound of short *u* in *put*, the broad *a* in *office*, and the short *u* in *bonnet*. Do not call *hundred* hŭn'derd, nor *scare* skēer.

Lesson 56.

NAMES OF FRUITS.

pe̸âr	pẽach	ăp'ple̸	chĕr'ry
plŭm	quĭnçe̸	lĕm'on	ŏr'anġe̸
līme̸	ġrāpe̸	mĕl'on	çĭt'ron

If a task is once begun,
Never leave it till it's done.

Lesson 57.

Sound of u and o before r, marked û and õ.

tûrn	ûr′chin	wõrt	wõr′thy
cûrb	ûr′ġent	wõrk	wõrld′ly
spûr	bûr′d∉n	wõrm	wõr′ship
cûrv∉	bûrġ′lar	wõrd	wõrm′wŏŏd

Lesson 58.

PROVERBS.

Never trouble trouble till trouble troubles you. To know that you know what you know, and to know that you do not know what you do not know,—that is true wisdom. Live in a worry, and death will hurry. He lives long that lives well; and time misspent is not lived, but lost.

Lesson 59.

WORDS OF OPPOSITE MEANINGS.

a bòv∉′	be lōẅ′	râr∉	cŏm′mon
noiṣ′y	quī′et	proud	hŭm′bl∉
ŏft′∉n	sĕl′dòm	wõrs∉	bĕt′ter
ŭp′per	lōẅ′er	elē∉n	dīrt′y
be fōr∉′	be hīnd′	brāv∉	tĭm′id

Lesson 60.

Sounds of **o** before *r*, like broad *a*, marked ô; and of **u** after *r*, like ōō, marked u̇.

eôrd'aġe̸	fôrt'ūne̸	bru̇'tal	pru̇'dent
eôr'net	môr'tal	eru̇'el	ru̇'in
dôr'mant	hôr'net	fru̇'ġal	ru̇'mor

Lesson 61.

What word in Lesson 60 means "destined to die"? Which refers to the ropes of a ship's rigging? Which means "sleeping"? Which signifies "careful"? Which is the name of an insect? Which, of a musical instrument?

Lesson 62.

NAMES OF ANIMALS AND THEIR YOUNG.

eow	eälf	hôrse̸	eōlt
ġōa̸t	kĭd	hĕn	chĭe̸k'en
be̸âr	eŭb	lī'on	whĕlp
dēe̸r	faẙn	eăt	kĭt'te̸n
shēe̸p	lămb̸	dŏġ	pŭp'py

Dare to do right; dare to be true.

ADDITIONAL WORDS.

Lesson 63.

Sounds before *r* of ĕ and ĭ.

hẽrd	pẽr'sŏn	sĭr	chĭrp
nẽrvĕ	hẽr'mit	dĭrt	çĭr'ċlĕ
sẽrvĕ	fẽr'tĭlĕ	fĭrst	kĭr'tlĕ
tẽrsĕ	fẽr'vent	shĭrt	ḡĭrd'lĕ
vẽrsĕ	mẽr'mājd	smĭrk	ĭrk'sŏmĕ

Lesson 64.

Sounds before *r* of û and ŏ.

eûrd	blûrt	sûr'loin	tûr'ban
fûrl	chûrn	mûr'der	tûr'bid
lûrk	eûrsĕ	mûr'mur	wŏrld
slûr	nûrsĕ	fûr'nish	wŏrst
tûrf	pûrsĕ	pûr'pōrt	wŏrth

Lesson 65.

Sounds of ô before *r* and ṳ after *r*.

eôrpsĕ	môr'sel	trṳĕ	rṳ'ral
fôr'ty	nôr'mal	prṳdĕ	ḡrṳ'el
ôr'der	sôr'did	frṳịt	trṳ'ant
eôr'ner	ḡôr'ḡĕŏŭs	crṳịṣĕ	ab strṳṣĕ'
bôr'der	tôr'por	erṳ'et	ex trṳdĕ'

SPELLER. 31

Lesson 66.

Italian sound of a, marked ä; and the broad sound, marked ạ.

är'bor	bär'lẹ̌y̆	ạl'so	wạ'ter
är'dent	bär'ter	bạl'sam	hạl'ter
är'g̃ụ̄ẹ́	eär'bon	lạụ́'rel	tạl̸k'er
ärm'or	eär'pet	fạl'ter	dạụ́g̸l̸'ter

Lesson 67.

REVIEW IN PRONUNCIATION.

The *a* in *orange* has the sound of short *e:* ŏr'enj. Both the *t* and *e* in *often* are silent: ŏf'n. The accent in *cornet* is on the first syllable. Webster pronounces *fortune* fôrt'yụn. *Calf* is not pronounced kăf, but käf,—*a* as in *arm*. *Water* and *daughter* are not pronounced wŏt'ter and dŏt'ter, but waw'ter and daw'ter.

Lesson 68.

NAMES OF FISHES.

eŏd	sōlẹ́	shăd	eärp	shärk
g̃är	chŭb	pīkẹ́	pērch	rō̸ach
rāy̸	dāçẹ́	bàss̸	trout	plā̸içẹ́

Goodness is beauty at its best.

Lesson 69.

Sounds of long o͞o, differently marked; **ew**, following *r*, has the same sound.

wh̥o	so͞up	rul̸e	bo͞om	drew
wh̥om	to͞ur	rud̸e	do͞om	g̅rew
lös̰e̸	cro͞up	crud̸e	lo͞on	crew
mo̤v̸ed	g̅ro͞up̸ed	brut̸e	blo͞om	screw

Lesson 70.

Sound of **n** like *ng*, marked n̰.

mĭn̰k	băn̰k	sŭn̰k	drăn̰k	ăn̰'g̅l̸e
rĭn̰k	lăn̰k	jŭn̰k	drŭn̰k	ăn̰'g̅er
sĭn̰k	blăn̰k	trŭn̰k	spŭn̰k	ŭn̰'cl̸e

Lesson 71.

SYNONYMS.

The equivalent words extend across the page.

ĕnd	ai̇m	bĕnt	scōp̸e	drĭft
sŏd	lȯa̸m	mōld	elŏd	c̄ạrth
fŭn	plāy̸	mīrth	spōrt	prăn̰k
rŏd	pōlc̦	eāṉe̸	stȧff̸	stĭc̸k

Sup wisely and you will sleep well.

SPELLER. 33

ADDITIONAL WORDS.

Lesson 72.

Sounds of ä and ạ.

bär′ber	bär′ḡain	baṉ′blẹ̸	ḡaẉk′y
ḡär′blẹ̸	eär′naḡẹ̸	eaṉ′eus	eaṉs′tie
jär′ḡon	där′ling	pạl′ter	maṉd′lin
mär′ḡin	pär′boil	paṉ′per	plaṉd′it
pär′çel	tär′nish	taẉ′dry	sạlt′nesṣ

Lesson 73.

Sounds of ọ, ụ, o͞o, and ew after r.

ḡroṉp	sprụçẹ̸	ḡro͞om	brew
roṉtẹ̸	trụ′isṃ	sho͞ot	shrew
whoṣẹ̸	hụr rä′	spo͞ol	strew
eoṉ′poṉ	trụf′flẹ̸	swo͞on	threw
ḡoṉr′mand	pro trụdẹ̸′	sno͞ozẹ̸	erew′el

Lesson 74.

Sound of ṉ before ḡ and k, and the k sounds of c, q, etc.

ăṉ′ḡry	brĭṉk	răṉ′eor	băṉ′quet
fĭṉ′ḡer	flăṉk	săṉe′tum	eŏṉ′quest
lăṉ′ḡuid	ăṉ′klẹ̸	fŭṉe′tion	văṉ′quish
eŏṉ′ḡresṣ	trĭṉk′et	săṉe′tion	mĭṉx
săṉ′ḡuĭṉẹ̸	sprĭṉk′lẹ̸	tĭṉet′ūrẹ̸	ăṉx′ĭẹ̸ŭs

P. S. B.—3.

Lesson 75.

Sharp sound of th, unmarked.

thĭn	pĭth	thŭn′der	pā′thos
thĭnk	truth	thou′ṣand	yøuth′fu̞l
thīng	dĕa̸th	thĭs′t̸le̸	thănk′fu̞l

Lesson 76.

Flat sound of th, marked th.

thĭs	brēa̸the̸	fä′ther	nôrth′ern
thĕm	smōōth	be nēa̸th′	søuth′ern
thou	blīthe̸	thĭth′er	thêre̸′fōre̸

Lesson 77.

To be copied, and placed on the board or slate.

Boys of spirit, boys of will,
Boys of muscle, brain, and power,
Fit to cope with any thing—
These are wanted every hour.

Lesson 78.

NAMES OF MEN.

John   Henry   Robert

James   Arthur   Thomas

Paul   Jacob   William

Frank   Charles   Richard

Lesson 79.

NAMES OF WOMEN.

Anna   Helen   Clara

Lucy   Edith   Alice

Ella   Mary   Agnes

Cora   Sarah   Laura

Lesson 80.

Sound of g like j, marked ġ.

ġĕm	ġĕn′der	ġĕst′ūrẹ	dān′ger
pāġẹ	ġĭn′ġer	o blīġẹ′	ġēn′iŭs
stāġẹ	ġĭb′bet	lŏġ′ie	ĕn′ġīnẹ
lĕḏġẹ	lē′ġend	măġ′ie	rē′ġion

Lesson 81.

Sound of g hard, marked ḡ.

ḡăḡ	ḡlōbẹ	ḡär′ter	fŏḡ′ḡy
ḡāvẹ	ḡrȧsp	ḡḫȧst′ly	erăḡ′ḡy
ḡāng	ḡrănd	ḡew′ḡa𝕨	lăḡ′ḡard
ḡôrḡẹ	ḡlȧnçẹ	ḡăl′lop	ḡĭḡ′ḡlẹ

Lesson 82.

SYNONYMS.

wīlẹ	rṳṣẹ	trĭçk	chēȧt	dŏḏġẹ
bĭt	jŏt	whĭt	mītẹ	serăp
coil	wĭnd	twīnẹ	twĭst	𝕨′rēȧth̬ẹ
vĕx	frĕt	chāfẹ	tẹḏṣẹ	plāḡṳẹ
tīẹ	lĭṉk	bŏnd	yōkẹ	chāĭn

Wile is an Anglo-Saxon word; **ruse** is French; **trick** is from the Dutch; **cheat** comes originally from the Latin; and **dodge** has been traced back to the north of England.

SPELLER.

ADDITIONAL WORDS.

Lesson 83.

Sound of th.

bōth	bērth	thĭrst	ăth'lētȩ
mŏth	fĭfth	thrĕa̤t	mĕth'od
ōa̤th	fa̤ith	thrīvȩ	ru̱th'lesȿ
ru̱th	smĭth	thwa̤rt	thrŏt'tlȩ

Sound of th.

thăn	līthȩ	ȯth'er	brȯth'er
thēȩ	tīthȩ	bŏth'er	smȯth'er
thēȿȩ	sōōthȩ	mȯth'er	fĕa̤th'er
thīnȩ	clōthȩ	răth'er	lĕa̤th'er

Lesson 84.

Sound of ġ.

pāġȩ	sĭnġȩ	brĭdġȩ	fräġ'ĭlȩ
rāġȩ	spȯnġȩ	lŏġ'ie	ġĭb'lets
sāġȩ	stāġȩ	măġ'ie	ȩon ġĕa̤l'
wāġȩ	tĭnġȩ	rĭġ'id	suḡ ġĕst'

Sound of ḡ.

flāḡ	măḡ'ḡot	brī ḡādȩ'	fa tīḡu̱ȩ'
prīḡ	dăḡ'ḡer	dī ḡrĕsȿ'	fräḡ'ment
snăḡ	ḡăl'ley	stăḡ'ḡer	smŭḡ'ḡler
be ġĭn'	sĭḡ'nal	ẉrĭḡ'ḡlȩ	strŭḡ'ḡlȩ

Lesson 85.

Long sound of y, marked ȳ.

lȳrȩ	al lȳ'	tȳ'ro	de crȳ'
tȳpȩ	de nȳ'	tȳ'rant	re plȳ'
stȳlȩ	re lȳ'	çȳ'elȩ	ap plȳ'
sȩȳthȩ	de fȳ'	hȳ'drant	com plȳ'

Lesson 86.

Short sound of y, marked y̆.

my̆th	ly̆r'ie	my̆s'tie	sy̆n'tax
ly̆nch	py̆ġ'my	ġy̆p'sum	phy̆ṣ'ie
ly̆mph	sy̆n'od	my̆th'ie	cry̆s'tal
try̆st	ġy̆p'sy	sy̆s'tem	sy̆mp'tom

Lesson 87.

Words pronounced alike. Copy the sentences below and fill the blanks with the proper words.

nŏt, ḵnŏt.—*He could —— tie a —— in the string.*

sŭm, sŏmȩ.—*He found the —— of —— of the numbers.*

bow, bougḥ.—*He had to ——— to go under the —— of the tree.*

fōrth, fōṵrth.—*He was the —— man to go —— to war.*

SPELLER. 39

Lesson 88.

SOUNDS OF CH.

Ch unmarked has nearly the sound of *tsh*, as in *much*.

sŭch	chē̱e̸r	chăp'ter	chăl'i̱ç̸e
whĭch	chĭd̸e	chăt't̸el	chär'nel
tē̱ach	chōk̸e	chăl'leṅġ̸e	chär'ter

Ch. as the sound of *k*, is marked in this book ϲh.

| ϲhrōin̸g | sϲhōol | ϲhā'os | sϲhŏl'ar |
| sϲhēm̸e | Ϲhrīst | ϲhrō'mo | sϲhōon'er |

Lesson 89.

WORDS OF SIMILAR MEANING.

slōw̸	tär'dy	fŏnd	lŏv'ing
snŭg	ē̱o'zy	rŏb	plŭn'der
răsh	hās'ty	rĭch	wĕ̱alth'y
ḡrĭm	sûr'ly	jŭst	ŭp'rīg̸ht
sōl̸e	sĭṉ'ġl̸e	hûrt	ĭn'jur̸e
sō̸ul	spĭr'it	lōōs̸e	un bound'

*The glories of our birth and state
Are shadows, not substantial things.*

ADDITIONAL WORDS.

Lesson 90.

Sound of ch.

mŭch	brōach	snătch	chām′ber
chärm	chānġe	strĕtch	chăt′ter
chĭn̲k	chûrch	chī′nȧ	chĭm′ney
dĭtch	prēach	chōṣ′en	săch′el
mătch	stĭtch	chĕr′ub	chief′tain

Sound of ch.

āche	trō′chē	chrŏn′ĭc	är′chīveṣ
lŏch	chŏl′er	dĭs′tich	tĕch′nics
chō′ral	chĕm′ist	schĕm′er	schĕd′ūle

Lesson 91.

Sound of ȳ.

plȳ	shȳ	drȳ′ad	eȳe′let
skȳ	drȳ	hȳ′brid	slȳ′ness
spȳ	sprȳ	hȳ′phen	stȳl′ish
trȳ	rhȳme	sup plȳ′	çȳ′press
whȳ	es pȳ′	shȳ′ness	ġȳ′rāte

Sound of y̆.

çy̆st	sy̆m′bol	rhy̆thm	sy̆l′van
ly̆n̲x	çy̆m′bal	hy̆s′sop	ġy̆m′nast
cry̆pt	ty̆m′bal	sy̆n′dic	sy̆r′in̲x

Lesson 92.

USE OF CAPITALS.

Begin with a capital letter every proper name, as *Paul, John Lothrop Motley*, or *New Mexico;* all words derived from proper names, as *Philadelphian, Japanese,* or *Irish;* titles of honor and respect, as *My dear Sir, His Excellency the Governor,* or *The Rev. J. A. Swaney, D. D.;* and all appellations of the Deity, as *God, Creator,* and *Redeemer.*

Lesson 93.

COMMON DUTIES OR ACTS PERFORMED.

fĭx	frȳ	chŏp	blŭsh	slēẹp
ēạt	hĕm	whĕt	bāthẹ	ḡrīnd
elēạn	sạẉ	dōzẹ	swēẹp	quĭlt
sŭp	kēẹp	fēẹd	brŭsh	tōạst
tĭp	wēẹp	tŭçk	wēạvẹ	shāvẹ
rĭp	mĕnd	quĭt	rōạst	skātẹ
mōẉ	rākẹ	lēạp	seour	fēạst
hōẹ	chăt	pēẹp	eärvẹ	mĭnçẹ
erȳ	chew	shŭt	märch	prụnẹ
prȳ	eōmḅ	lŏḷḷ	slīçẹ	stămp

Which six of the above words apply to farm-work? Which five to sewing? Which five to cooking? Form sentences including these.

Lesson 94.

WORDS OF THREE SYLLABLES.

Long and short sounds of the vowels.

bā'by hōŏd	dē'i ty	pī'e ty
pā'tri ot	ē'ḡo tĭst	vī'o lent
răt'i fȳ	bĕn'e fit	hĭs'to ry
văl'en tĭnǥ	ĕl'e ment	mĭn'is ter
ō'di um	fū'ner al	hȳ ē'nȧ
pō'et ry	mū'ti ny	dȳ'nam ītǥ
mŏd'est y	sŭb'sė quent	hȳp'o erītǥ
pŏs'si blǥ	eūl'ti vātǥ	mȳs'ti fȳ

Lesson 95.

EXERCISES ON THE ABOVE LESSON.

We *ratify* an agreement when we approve or sanction it; we *mystify* when we perplex or involve one in mystery. A *patriot* is one who loves his country; an *egotist* loves himself, and is often lacking in *modesty*. A *hypocrite* is one who assumes an appearance of *piety*, which should subject him to the *odium* of good men. *History* is a record of the past; *babyhood* is the state of being a baby; and a *hyena* is a wild beast. The mind is *cultivated* by labor, care, and study.

Lesson 96.

SOUNDS OF C.

Soft sound of c, marked ç.

dīçe̸	çēa̸se̸	çī'der	ăç'id
twīçe̸	trāçe̸	çĕn'sus	tăç'it

Hard sound of c, marked c.

tăc'tic	vīc'tor	cŏp'per	cŏm'ic
hĕc'tic	nĕc'tar	căn'dle̸	stūe'co

In these words the unmarked c is sounded like z.

suf fīce̸'   diṣ cērn'   săe'ri fīce̸

In these words the canceled c is silent.

e̸zür   vi¢t'u̸alṣ   in di¢t'ment

Lesson 97.

Sounds of ie and ei as long ē.

sīeġe̸	fīeld	wēi̸r	con çēi̸t'
fīend	yīeld	sēize̸	de çēi̸t'
brīef	wīeld	wēi̸rd	de çēi̸ve̸'
thīef	chīef	shīeld	re līeve̸'

N. B.—In words of this kind e usually follows c, and i follows l.

Lesson 98.

SOUNDS OF X.

The regular sharp sound of x, like *ks*, is unmarked.

wăx	ĕx'it	ex pĕnd'	ex pẽrt'
flăx	ĕx'īlę́	ex pĕet'	sĕx'ton
nĕxt	tĕxt'ūrę́	ex pīrę́'	dĕx'ter

Soft sound of x like *gz*, marked x̣.

ex̣ äet'	ex̣ īst'	ex̣ õrt'	ex̣ ĕmp̣t'
ex̣ ạlt'	ex̣ ŭlt'	ex̣ hôrt'	ex̣ hạṵst'

Exercise.—The *sexton* *exhorted* the *exile* to make his *exit*. To *exist* is to *be;* to *exult* is to *rejoice;* and to *expire* is to *die.*

Lesson 99.

WORDS PERTAINING TO MOTION OF VARIOUS KINDS.

rŭn	rēęl	dȧnçę́	shākę́	strāy̆
hŏp	spin	wạltz	hēạvę́	slīdę́
flȳ	mọvę́	hāstę́	trḝ̆ạd	seālę́
stĭr	rōḷ!'	spēę́d	trămp	mount
pȧss	rŏc̣k	quĭc̣k	märch	flēę́t
skĭp	stĕp	swĭft	erēę́p	strōll'
lēạp	rŭsh	whĭrl	erạy̆'l	bounçę́
trŏt	jŭmp	twĭrl	flōặt	prȧnçę́
flĭt	rōạm	quākę́	glīdę́	sprĭng

SPELLER. 45

Lesson 100.

The sound of s like z, marked ṣ.

ēᶊ'ṣy   tăn'ṣy   nā'ṣal   pre ṣūmᶒ'
eḵásm   mī'ṣer   re ṣŭlt'   deṣ ṣērt'
blouṣᵉ   rĕṣ'in   plĕᶏṣ'ant   diṣ ṣŏlvᵉ'

In the following words y and i are *consonants*.

yĕlᶌ   yŏn'der   āl'ien   elōth'ier
yärn   yĕᶇr'ly   ūn'ion   eōᶈrt'ier
yᵒuth   yᵉō'man   mĭn'ion   brĭlᶌ'iant

Malice toward none; charity for all.

Lesson 101.

PARTS OF A HOUSE.

hạlᶌ   dōør   çĕl'lar   çĕᶅ'ing
roof   pŏrch   lĭn'tel   wĭn'dōẃṣ
sĭlᶌ   stâᶎrṣ   ḡär·'ret   chĭm'nᵉȳṣ
săsh   rōōmṣ   pär'lor   shŭt'terṣ
ĕᶏvᵉṣ   frāmᵉ   păn'try   kĭᶄch'en
wạllᶊ   ḡä'blᵉ   elŏṣ'et   wạᶎn'seot
stĕps   joists   eôr'nĭçᵉ   wạrd'rōbᵉ
spout   hᵉärths   măn'tᵉlṣ   chăm'berṣ
flōør   ăt'tie   trăn'sóm   thrĕsh'ōld

Lesson 102.

Verbs in which the final d is sounded like t.

waḷkęd	swĭṭchęd	ḡrāçęd	märchęd
washęd	y̌rĕnchęd	erŭshęd	măṭchęd
warpęd	elŭṭchęd	serāpęd	skĕṭchęd
eûrsęd	blĕsşęd	pē͏̆akęd	seôrchęd

Adjectives in which ed is sounded.

ā'ġed	erăb'bed	lēȧrn'ed	wĭçk'ed
blĕsş'ed	stŭb'bed	be lóv'ed	dŏḡ'ḡed
eûrs'ed	pē͏̆ak'ed	jăḡ'ḡed	rŭḡ'ḡed

Lesson 103.

SYNONYMS.

ENGLISH.	LATIN.	ENGLISH	LATIN.
āpę́	ĭm'i tātę́	bōld	văl'or ǿus
lŏvę́	af fĕe'tion	lĭft	čl'e vātę́
tāmę́	do mĕs'tie	rousę́	aġ'i tātę́
wīld	fe rō'ciǿūs	strĕss	ĕm'pha sĭs

My strength is as the strength of ten;

Because my heart is pure.

SPELLER. 47

ADDITIONAL WORDS.

Lesson 104.

Sounds of ç and c.

brȧçȩ	dc çīdȩ'	eā'blȩ	ae erṳȩ'
prīnçȩ	po līçȩ'	ăet'īvȩ	bro eādȩ'
thrīçȩ	sc çēdȩ'	rěe'tor	eon erētȩ'
çĕm'ent	lī'çensȩ	vīe'tim	pre elūdȩ'
çĭs'tern	ro mănçȩ'	tăe'ties	re erṳit'

Lesson 105.

Sounds of ie and ei = ē.

nïeçȩ	prïest	bïer	sēïz'ūrȩ
fïērçȩ	be lïef'	tïer	per çēïvȩ'
pïērçȩ	be sïege'	shrïek	re çēïpt'
grïēvȩ	re prïevȩ'	shēïk	sēïgn'ior
thïēvȩ	re trïevȩ'	sēïnȩ	de çēit'ful

Lesson 106.

Sounds of x and x̱.

bŭx'om	ex çĕl'	ex̱ ūdȩ'	eō ex̱ ïst'
vĭx'ȩn	ex çīte'	ex̱ ŏt'ie	ex̱ ĕm'plar
wăx'ȩn	ex plāïn'	ex̱ ăm'ïnȩ	ex̱ ĕmp'tion
ĕx'tant	ex tīnet'	ex̱ ẽr'tion	ex̱ ïst'ençȩ
eŏx'eōmb	ex trēmȩ'	ex̱ hīb'it	ex̱ haust'ion

ADDITIONAL WORDS.

Lesson 107.

Sounds of ṣ.

älmṣ	rāịṣé	rōṣ'y	pĕ**ạ**ṣ'ant
hōṣé	choōṣé	păn'ṣy	vīṣ'it
rīṣé	prāịṣé	hŭṣ'ṣy	eǿŭṣ'ỵ̆n
wīṣé	plēạṣé	flĭm'ṣy	prĭṣ'ǿn
elōṣé	spăṣm	ḡrēạ̣ṣ'y	hŭṣ'band
pạ**ụ**ṣé	trădę́ṣ	ex eūṣé'	prĕṣ'ençé

Lesson 108.

Y a consonant.

yŏn	yĕlp	Yăṉ'keé	be yŏnd'
yĕlk	yēạ̣rn	yĕs'ter daў	hăl'yard

Lesson 109.

I a consonant.

ȯn'ion	mŭll̓'ion	bụll̓'ion	pe eūl'iar
bŭn'ion	pĭll̓'ion	Sāv'ior	be hāv'ior
pĭn'ion	seŭll̓'ion	pŏn'iard	eo tīl'ion
mĭll̓'ion	trŭnịí'ion	spăn'iel	re bĕll'ion
bĭll̓'ion	quĕs'tion	eȯll̓'ier	eom păn'ion
trĭll̓'ion	€ḥŕĭs'tian	fŭs'tian	me dăll'ion

Lesson 110.

T and s before *io* usually have the sound of *sh*.

nā′tion	ăe′tion	měn′tion	pěn′sion
rā′tion	nō′tion	díe′tion	těn′sion
stā′tion	ŏp′tion	aɟte′tion	măn′sion

In some words **ci** has the sound of *sh*.

spē′cie	g̈lā′cial	spē′ciēs̱	g̈rā′ciøŭs
sō′cial	spĕ′cial	eru̱′cial	prĕ′ciøŭs

The following words represent other forms of the sound *sh*.

sȼhĭst	nŏx′iøŭs	ɇŏn′sciøŭs	lŭx′ū ry
ō′cean	naɟt′seøŭs	fĭs′sūrɇ	su̱g̈′ar

Lesson 111.

WORDS PERTAINING TO MUSIC.

âɟr	sŏng	shärp	trī′o	g̈ăm′ut
lāy̸	tūnɇ	eɟtôrd	ăl′to	mū′s̱ie
ełĕf	tōnɇ	voiçɇ	dĭt′ty	těn′or
flăt	nōtɇ	sō′lo	vō′eal	băl′lad
sĭng	stȧff̸	du ĕt′	strāɟn	eɟtō′rus

An inch an hour, a foot a day.

P. S. B.—4.

ADDITIONAL WORDS.

Lesson 112.

Sound of ti like sh.

pō'tion   jŭne'tion   o rā'tion
mō'tion   făe'tiøŭs   ere ā'tion
eăp'tion   frăe'tiøŭs   do nā'tion
făe'tion   quō'tient   du rā'tion
eaµ'tion   sĕn'ti ent   ḡra dā'tion
fīe'tion   pā'tiençø   mu nĭ'tion

Lesson 113.

Sounds of ṣi like zh, and si like sh.

ō'ṣier   tôr'sion   ae çĕs'sion
hō'ṣier   çĕs'sion   ad mĭs'sion
brā'ṣier   sĕs'sion   de elĕn'sion
fū'ṣion   vẽr'sion   eon çũs'sion
suā'ṣion   trăn'sient   ex prĕs'sion

Lesson 114.

Sound of ci like sh.

lŭs'ciøŭs   Ḡrē'cian   ma lī'ciøŭs
spā'ciøŭs   ju dī'cial   suf fĭ'cient
spē'ciøŭs   mu ṣī'cian   sus pĭ'cion
eŏn'ꞩciençø   ma ḡī'cian   te nā'ciøŭs

SPELLER. 51

Lesson 115.

IRREGULAR SOUNDS OF VOWELS.

Unmarked vowels sounded like short ĕ.

a'ny	bur'y	mĕn'açẹ́	˙pās'sag̣ẹ́
said	man'y	môrt̄'g̣ag̣ẹ́	sŏl'açẹ́
says̱	a g̱ain'	prĕf'açẹ́	răv'ag̣ẹ́
saith	a g̱ainst'	tĕr'raçẹ́	saụ̈'sag̣ẹ́

Unmarked vowels sounded like short ĭ.

| been | lĕt'tuçẹ́ | ₍pret'ty | ₎breech'e̱s̱ |
| bus̱'y | ₍wom'en | ₎En̲'g̱lish | bus̱'ines̱s̱ |

Lesson 116.

VERBS DISTINGUISHED.

In the use of the following words careful discrimination should be observed. Examples should be given by the teacher on all, and the pupil guarded against their abuse.

g̱ụ̈es̱s̱   ex pĕet'   in tĕnd'   pûr'pȯsẹ́   mis trŭst'
douḅt   rĕc̱k'ọ́n   be lïevẹ́'   sus pĕet'   eăl'eu lātẹ́

Expect has always a reference to the future; hence it is improper to say, "I *expect* the mail has arrived." What should be said is: "I *think* (or *believe*) the mail has arrived." As **guess** means to *conjecture* or *imagine*, and **reckon** to *compute*, it would be equally improper to say, "I *reckon* (or *guess*) the mail has arrived." Neither does **calculate** mean *intend* or *purpose;* hence it is improper to say, "He *calculates* to go on a journey." **Suspect** means to *mistrust*, and is not a synonym for *expect*.

Lesson 117.

SOUNDS OF OUGH AND AUGH.

In the following **gh** is sounded like *f*.

laugh	rough	sough	e nough'
cough	tough	trough	draught

In the following **gh** is silent.

dough	bough	taught	sought
though	plough	caught	bought
bor'ough	drought	naught	fought
thor'ough	dough'ty	fraught	nought
fur'lough	through	haugh'ty	thought

Lesson 118.

EXPLANATIONS OF THE ABOVE LESSON.

Sough is a sighing sound, as of wind in trees. *Draught* is also spelled draft, and the latter orthography is more generally used in military and commercial circles. *Slough*, meaning the part that separates from a foul sore, is pronounced sluf; as a miry place, slou; in the Central states the latter is called slōō. *Plough* is now more generally spelled plow. *Drought*, want of rain, has taken the place of *drouth*, and *naught* is now less frequently written *nought*.

Lesson 119.

Words in which qu is sounded like k, marked qu̸

pïqu̸e̸	eo qu̸ĕt' (v.)	eŏn'qu̸er	eo qu̸ĕtt̸e̸' (n.)
bisqu̸e̸	ero qu̸e̱t'	pïqu̸'ant	an tïqu̸e̸'
elïqu̸e̸	bou̸ qu̸e̱t'	par qu̸e̱t'	tur qu̸ois̱'
plăqu̸e̸	liq'u̸ór	ob lïqu̸e̸'	bur lĕsqu̸e̸'

Words in which t is silent.

fàst̸'e̸n	eăs'tl̸e̸	brĭs'tl̸e̸	eḧris't̸e̸n
hăs't̸e̸n	nĕst̸'l̸e̸	chās't̸e̸n	nĕst̸'ling
lĭst̸'e̸n	hŭs'tl̸e̸	glĭs't̸e̸n	chĕst̸'nut
sŏft̸'e̸n	grĭs'tl̸e̸	moist̸'e̸n	a pŏs'tl̸e̸

Lesson 120.

SYNONYMS DISTINGUISHED.

ae çĕpt', re çĕi̸v̸e̸'.—*We* receive *news when it reaches us; we* accept *presents when offered.*

ae eŏm'plish, ef fĕet', ĕx'e eūt̸e̸, a chĩēv̸e̸', perfôrm'.—*We* accomplish *an end; we* effect *a purpose; we* execute *a design; we* perform *a task; and we* achieve *an undertaking of importance.*

aw̸'ful, frīght'ful, drĕa̸d'ful.—*An accident may be* frightful; *the approach of death is* dreadful *to most men; the convulsions of an earthquake are* awful, *because filling us with awe.*

Lesson 121.

Words in which k, g, or n is silent.

knăb	knăck	gnăt	de sīgn'
knew	sīgn	gnaw	poign'ant
knēel	im pūgn'	gnärl	sŏl'emn
knăp'săck	ma līgn'	gnăsh	cŏl'umn
knŏwl'edge	for'eign	gnōme	con děmn'

Lesson 122.

Words in which b, l, s, h, or w is silent.

děbt	hälf	hērb	wrěck
dŭmb	pälm	ghōst	wrēath
nŭmb	stalk	rhěum	wrěnch
re doubt'	isl'and	ghast'ly	wrăn'gle
sŭbt'le	vis'count	rhu'bärb	wrink'le

Lesson 123.

Words in which ph is sounded like f.

phrāse	nymph	dŏl'phin	ĕp'i tăph
phlěgm	ôr'phan	sŭl'phur	ĕl'e phant
phŏn'ic	sī'phon	săp'phire	phā'e tŏn
phěas'ant	něph'ew	phā'lanx	de çī'pher
phăn'tasm	prŏph'et	păm'phlet	phy si'cian

SPELLER. 55

Lesson 124.

SPECIAL DRILL IN PRONUNCIATION.

One vague inflection fills the soul with doubt;
One trivial letter ruins all left out;
A *knot* can choke a felon into clay;
A *not* will save him, spelt without the *k*;
The smallest word has some unguarded spot,
And danger lurks in *i* without a dot.

The following words are to be especially guarded against—
they are pronounced differently, but are often confounded in
common speech: năp, năp𝑒̸; ŏf (ŏv), ŏf𝑓̸; wạnt, wōn't, wȯnt;
găp, găp𝑒̸; wĭth, wĭth𝑒̸; eănt, eän't; ä𝑛̸nt, ȧnt; nĭ𝑒̸k, nĭch𝑒̸;
newş (nūş), n͞o͞oş𝑒̸; ē𝑎̸st, yē𝑎̸st; seăth, seāth𝑒̸; lō𝑎̸th, lō𝑎̸th𝑒̸;
hăv𝑒̸, hä𝑙̸v𝑒̸; ĭ𝑐̸ch, ē𝑎̸ch; ŏn, ạ𝑤̸n; sȧt, sōt; G͞od, gạ𝑢̸d; nŏd,
𝑔̸nạ𝑤̸𝑒̸d; sōd, sạ𝑤̸𝑒̸d; dōn, dạ𝑤̸n.

Lesson 125.

Give the short sound to **a** in these words.

băd𝑒̸	măt'in	tăs'sel	păġ'𝑔̸ant
străp	lī'lae	săt'ĭr𝑒̸	năr'rōẉ
stămp	răp'ĭn𝑒̸	Ăr'ab	al tēr'nat𝑒̸ (adj.)
eă𝑡̸ch	hăr'assˢ	băr'rel	ăl'ter nāt𝑒̸ (v.)

Give the short sound to **e** in these words.

ġĕt	tĕn'et	tĕt'ter	trĕb'l𝑒̸
yĕt	tĕp'id	kĕt'tl𝑒̸	dĕe'ad𝑒̸
lĕst	fĕt'id	pĕd'ant	whĕth'er
dĕj𝑡̸ĭ	ĕp'oeḵ	for ġĕt'	ẉrĕs'𝑡̸l𝑒̸

Lesson 126.

Short sound of i.

rĭd	vĭş'or	tĭ rādę'	trĭb'ūnę
rĭnsę	sĭr'up	fū'tĭlę	prō'fĭlę
wĭdth	ŏx'ĭdę	Ā'prĭl	fī nănçę'
vĭe'ar	dĭ lātę'	dĭ vĕst'	rĕs'pĭtę

Short sound of o and u.

slŏth	prŏç'esş	prŏv'òst	dŭe'at
dŏṉ'kęў	prŏḡ'resş	frŏnt'ı̈er	sŭp'plę
pŏl'len	be trŏth'	dŏç'ĭlę	pŭp'pet
ḡrŏv'ęl	prŏd'ūçę	jŏe'und	fŭl'sòmę

Lesson 127.

Long sound of a.

yęā	lä'mà	ḡrā'tis	sā'li ent
jęān	dāı̇́'ry	ān'cient	to mā'to
ā'pex	pā'tron	rā'tionş	sa ḡā'cięŭs
bä'bel	mā'tron	squā'lôr	ra pā'cięŭs

Long sound of e.

rēạr	sē'nĭlę	çērę'ment	sē'rı̈ēş
slēęk	ef fētę'	trēạ'elę	fū'brĭlę
lē'ver	lēı̇́'şūrę	prē'lūdę	lē'ġend
elïqµę	ēı̇́'ther	stēęl'yard	nēı̇́'ther

Lesson 128.

Long sound of i.

shīrɇ	sī'ren	vī'rīlɇ	ɇär'bīnɇ
tī'ny	grīm'y	fī'nītɇ	quī'nīnɇ

Long sound of o.

fōrġɇ	re vōlt'	ō'zōnɇ	flō'rist
ōn'ly	trō'phy	ĭn'mōst	fōr'ġer

Long sound of u.

lɨɇū	dū'ty	lū'rid	flū'ent

Lesson 129.

Words properly pronounced in two syllables.

lĭ'en	eāɨs'son	ġēn'ius	tĭɇk'lish
jăvɇ'lin	rŭff'ian	ġrɨēv'ɇŭs	jūn'ior
heɨ'nɇŭs	fĭl'ial	bĭv'ɇuāe	brĕth'ren

Words properly pronounced in three syllables.

ĭ dē'à	rĕġ'ū lar	pre vĕnt'ĭvɇ
jō'vi al	vĭe'to ry	plā'ġɨa rĭṣm
eôr'di al	hȳ'ġi ēnɇ	mēl'ior ātɇ
trĭv'i al	ē'vɇn ing	un lēɑ́rn'ed
ġē'ni al	eär'ri on	al lē'ġɨançɇ

GENERAL REVIEW OF SOUNDS.

Lesson 130.

lăçk	çĕnt	fĭlm	erŏp
băng	dĕad	ḡĭft	eŏçk
hăsh	hĕlp	hĭlt	bŭlb
răpt	tĕst	kĭng	fŭnd
sănk	kĕpt	mĭlk	ḡŭlp
măsh	tĕxt	wĭçk	tŭft

Lesson 131.

cräpe	blēak	brīde	brōke
flāme	blēed	erīed	erōak
shāpe	trēat	whīte	shōne
trāin	stēed	flīght	ḡlōat
sāint	snēak	spīte	seōld
tāste	creām	sprīght	hōard

Lesson 132.

quoit	heärt	swạrd	brạwl
cloud	härm	seạld	flạsk
flour	pärse	seôrch	ḡrạnt
mouth	snärl	ḡaụze	blạnch
prowl	stärve	claụse	trạnce
pounçe	läunch	sprạwl	stạnch

REVIEW. (Continued.)

Lesson 133.

jẽrk	fẽrn	swạsh	rọu̸g̸
dĩrk	bûrn	ḡrı̸ef	rōost
bûr	bĩrch	lı̸eġ̸	sōoth
whĩr	lẽa̸rn	frı̸ēz̸	stōop
wẽr̸	dûrst	pı̸ēç̸d	swōop
blûr	quĩrk	tı̸ẽrç̸	whōop

Lesson 134.

clin̤k	swạth	erı̆nġ̸	twı̆nġ̸
plăn̤k	swāth̸	drŭdġ̸	shrŭḡ
shrŭn̤k	shĕa̸th̸	frı̆nġ̸	slŭng
sphı̆n̤x	thŏs̸	hĕdġ̸	sprăng
thăn̤k	thĩrd	plŭnġ̸	vōḡu̸̸
quōth	thĕnç̸	trŭdġ̸	strĕngth

Lesson 135.

bŭnch	quĕnch	ch̸ȳm̸	hĕnç̸
fĕtch	ḉhāı̸s̸	onç̸	sē̸th̸
c̸ouch	chās̸d	pŭls̸	sçēn̸
hătch	chāst̸	fōrç̸	c̸lăn̤k
serē̸ch	c̸ōn̤ek̸	erēa̸s̸	kĕdġ̸
serătch	ch̸ȳl̸	flē̸ç̸	eătch

REVIEW. (Continued.)

Lesson 136.

skĭff̸	ₑrouch	blĕnd	slāy̸
serĭpt	seămp	frᵢ̃end	slei̸gh̸
skĭrt	skĕtch	frei̸gh̸t	ġĭst
seout	Seŏtch	trāi̸t	jĕst
skŭlk	sĭ₵v₵	nāy̸	tīm₵
seowl	ei̸gh̸th	nei̸gh̸	th̸ȳm₵

Lesson 137.

bāi̸z₵	ḡrāz₵	thȳ	k̸nē₵
prāi̸s₵	prĭṣm	thĭgh̸	nĭgh̸
blāz₵	snē₵z₵	quīt₵	ǵnärl
browṣ₵	spouṣ₵	blīgh̸t	ₑrŭmb̸
frōz₵	seø̸ûrġ₵	trīt₵	quäl̸m
prōṣ₵	strāi̸gh̸t	sīgh̸t	k̸nōy̸n

Lesson 138.

brāi̸n	ĕdġ₵	lēa̸st	serē₵n
blēa̸ch	hĭnġ₵	quāi̸nt	serēa̸m
blŏtch	hĭtch	plăi̸d	whēa̸t
ₑlŭtch	hŭnch	lûrch	thŭmb̸
dēa̸rth	drĕa̸d	sēa̸rch	warmth
ₑlēa̸nṣ₵	dămp̸ₑ̸d	plŭmb̸	wrôi̸gh̸t

SPELLER. 61

REVIEW. (*Continued.*)

Lesson 139.

fĭg'ūrḝ	frĭg'id	dāḭ'ly	trēḁ'ty
clăn̄'gor	fĭd'ġet	ōẉ'ing	sōl'dier
stŏm'acḫ	stĕr'ĭlḝ	rēḁ'ṣǿn	hēḁ'thḝn
vĕs'tĭġḝ	frăet'ūrḝ	trī'flḝ	nḝū'tral
hŏs'taġḝ	flǿŭr'ish	ăeḫ'ing	trī'umph
dŭn'ġḝon	bŭs'ṯler	fḝūd'al	fā'cial

Lesson 140.

ăx'lḝ	elēr'ġy	rāḭ'ṣḭn	shŏp'ping
ēḁ'ṣḝl	stûr'dy	chär'ġer	joint'ūrḝ
aṉ'thor	nērv'ǿŭs	jǿûr'nal	trăn̄'quil
rē'ġḭon	hĭth'er	chăp'lḁin	ser'ġeḁnt
buoy'ant	băp'tiṣm	rōġṉ'ish	lăn̄'guaġḝ
çōg'nac	kĭnṣ'fōḻk	ẉrĕsṯ'ling	prē'çin̄et

Lesson 141.

de fēr'	ac çēdḝ'	con çẽrn'	ex pĕnsḝ'
de mûr'	ex çḝḝd'	sue çĕsṣ'	ap pēḁsḝ'
ex çĕsṣ'	as çĕnd'	pre dīet'	af flīet'
ex hūmḝ'	re ṣçīnd'	diṣ dāḭn'	ac eûrsḝ'
in çīṣḝ'	a skănçḝ'	eam pāḭġn'	as pērsḝ'
con fūṣḝ'	con elūdḝ'	cŏn'struḝ	ero quĕtṯḝ'

REVIEW. (Continued.)

Lesson 142.

jew'el	fū'el	tow'el	vow'el
fĭꞇk'lꞇ	eăv'il	bŭꞇk'lꞇ	dꞇūb'lꞇ
rŭs'ꞇlꞇ	fū'ṣil	bŭs'ꞇlꞇ	tĭn'sel
mŭs'çlꞇ	trĕs'ꞇlꞇ	săn'dal	chăn'çel
jŏs'ꞇlꞇ	fŏnd'lꞇ	serĭb'blꞇ	wēạ'ṣꞇl
mĭs'sal	tŭn'nel	trăm'mel	whĭs'ꞇlꞇ

Lesson 143.

pur sūꞇ'	re trēạt'	o beỵ'	ḡa zĕtꞇꞇ'
per tāịn'	eom plētꞇ'	in veịḡḳ'	in trĭḡụꞇ'
pur veỵ'	re môrsꞇ'	em prīṣꞇ'	o pāqụꞇ'
per hăps'	dis eōụrsꞇ'	bap tīzꞇ'	qua drĭllꞇ'
pur loin'	re hẽạrsꞇ'	ea rēꞇn'	ḡro tĕsqụꞇ'
per chànçꞇ'	dis bûrsꞇ'	eon vēnꞇ'	ḡa zĕllꞇ'

Lesson 144.

sạụ'çer	sẽr'mon	wēạk'nesṣ	squir'rel
sạỵ'yer	çẽr'tịặin	wēꞇk'-dāỵ'	tôr'tꞇịsḝ
rꞇŭf'ꞇlꞇ	çĭr'eụịt	tẽrsꞇ'lỵ	sue çịṇet'
rꞇŭgh'nesṣ	sẽrv'īlꞇ	tur moil'	tab leau'
sĕn'tençꞇ	sûr'plus	stū'por	mŏn'strꞇŭs
çẽn'surꞇ	sûr'plịçe	stew'ard	dĭph'thong

SPELLER. 63

REVIEW. (Continued.)

Lesson 145.

mē′te or	pŏl′i ties	bu̱l′le tin
lā′bor er	pŏl′y ḡŏn	a̱n̴′to ḡrăph
eō′ḡen çy	fĕs′ti val	mēr′ean tĭl𝜙
ăd′jee tĭv𝜙	mĭr′a el𝜙	ôr′el̴es trȧ
eăt′ȧ lŏḡn̴𝜙	är′se nal	qua̱n′ti ty
mĭs′chiev 𝜙ŭs	pär′ti el𝜙	roy′al ty

Lesson 146.

ap prāi̴ş′al	a dŏp′tion	ab sôrb′ent
pro fū′şion	as çĕn′sion	ae eount′ant
eom mō′tion	eon trăe′tion	un däṉt′ed
as pīr′ant	fu̱l fĭl̴′ment	dĭ vẽr′sion
ea thē′dral	sub stăn′tial	ma çhĭn′ist
in ḡēn′i𝜙ŭs	eom pŭl′sion	re lin̠′quish

Lesson 147.

ăp per tāi̴n′	ăp ro pōş′	sŭb ma rĭn𝜙′
as çer tāi̴n′	ĭm po līt𝜙′	ĭn ter rŭpt′
brĭḡ a dīer′	çhăn de lier′	ae quĭ ĕşç𝜙′
pēr se vẽr𝜙′	ĕt i quĕtt𝜙′	çĭr eum vŏlv𝜙′
ĕn ḡi nēer′	eŏm′plai̴ şănç𝜙	ap pre hĕnd′
ŏp por tūn𝜙′	ĕf fer vĕşç𝜙′	pĭet ūr ĕsqn̴𝜙′

Lessons 148 and 149.

MARKS USED IN WRITING AND PRINTING.

— dăsh, *denotes a sudden pause.*
˘ brĕvĕ, *short sounds of vowels.*
{ brāçĕ, *connects words or lines.*
~ tĭl'de, *placed over* ñ, *to show that a consonant sound is added.*
. pē'ri od, *a full stop.*
, cŏm'mȧ, *a short pause.*
¯ mā'cron, *long sounds of vowels.*
☞ ĭn'dex, *that which points out, or invites attention.*
: cō'lon, *pause less than a period.*
∧ eā'ret, *shows an omission.*
- hȳ'phen, *connects syllables or lines; a mark somewhat similar put under* n, *sounded as* ng, *is called a* **bar,** *while in* s *or* x *it is called a* **suspended bar.** *Placed under* e *it gives the sound of* ā, *as in* feint (fānt).
* * * } el lĭp'sis, *marks showing that something is omitted.*
. . . }
" " quo tā'tion märks, *inclose something quoted.*
¶ păr'a ḡrăph, *used as a reference, or to mark a division.*
* ăs'ter ĭsk, ⎫
‡ sĕc'tion, ⎪ These marks are
† dăḡ'ger, ⎬ used to refer
‡ dŏub'lĕ ⎪ to passages or
   dăḡ'ger, ⎪ notes in the
‖ păr'al lels. ⎭ margin, or to foot-notes.

¨ dī ær'e sĭs, *placed over the second of two vowels to show that they are to be pronounced as distinct letters. Also used as a diacritical mark, as* ä *in* arm, *and called* **dots.** *In* ănt *it is called a* **dot.** *(See Lessons 20 and 43.)*
[ ] brăçk'ets, *or* erŏtch'ets, *used to inclose an explanation, reference, or note.*
^ *or* ~ çĭr'cum flĕx, *used to indicate certain vowel sounds, as* â *in* air. *[The* ĭ *in* bird *is marked by a* circumflex*—sometimes called a* wave.*]*
ˏ çe dĭl'lȧ, *placed under* ç, *to show that it is sounded like* s.
' a pŏs'tro phe, *denotes the omission of a letter or letters; also the possessive case: as,* John's.
; sĕm'i cō lon, *a pause of longer duration than a comma.*
! ĕx cla mā'tion point, *shows surprise or wonder.*
? in tĕr ro ḡā'tion point, *expresses doubt, or asks a question: as,* Who knows?
( ) pa rĕn'the sĭs, *incloses something inserted, by way of explanation, within another sentence. Dashes serve the same end.*

N. B.—In writing, italics are indicated by *one* line drawn underneath the word, small capitals by *two* lines, and capitals by *three*.

PART II.—ORTHOGRAPHY.

In this department will be found some general rules for the spelling of certain classes of words, with illustrations and exceptions. The forming of words into lesson-groups, with a view to their definition, is continued, and other features are added.

Lesson 150.

The letters **f, l,** and **s,** at the end of monosyllables, and standing immediately after single vowels, are generally doubled.

găff	chảff	wạll	lăss	glăss
dŏff	elĭff	dĕll	mĕss	prĕss
pŭff	stŭff	hĭll	hĭss	blĭss
bŭff	snŭff	dŏll	mŏss	grōss
cŭff	stĭff	lŭll	fŭss	trŭss
lŭff	scŏff	fĕll	kĭss	drŏss

Exceptions to the above rule.

ĭf	ăs	găs	hĭs	elĕf
ĭs	ŭs	hăs	yĕs	thŭs
ŏf	sŏl	wạs	pŭs	plŭs

The following are the only other common words, ending with other consonants than *f, l,* and *s,* which double their finals.

ăbb	ŏdd	ērr	ĭnn	mĭtt
ĕbb	ĕgg	ădd	fĭzz	bŭzz

Lesson 151.

Words formed by adding a termination beginning with a vowel to monosyllables, or words accented on the last syllable, usually double the final consonant if the primary word ends in a single consonant preceded by a single vowel.

pĕġġĕd	săd'dest	in fĕr̃r̃ĕd'
drŏppĕd	hŏt'test	a bĕt'ted
elĭppĕd	băġ'ġaġĕ	be ġĭn'ner

Some exceptions to the above rule.

| çha ġrĭnĕd' | prĕf'er ençĕ | chȧn'çel lor |
| dĕf'er ençĕ | rĕf'er ençĕ | erȳs'tal līzĕ |

Lesson 152.

HOMOPHONOUS WORDS.

Copy the exercises below and fill the blanks.

āi̯l, *to be sick.*
āle̸, *a kind of liquor.*
āi̯t, *an island.*
āte̸, *did eat.*
ei̯ġht, *a number.*
bāi̯l, *surety.*
bāle̸, *a bundle.*
bāi̯t, *an allurement.*
bāte̸, *to lessen.*

fai̯n, *gladly.*
fāne̸, *a temple.*
fei̯ġn, *to pretend.*
pāi̯l, *a bucket.*
pāle̸, *whitish; dim.*
tāi̯l, *an appendage.*
tāle̸, *a story.*
wāi̯l, *to lament.*
wāle̸, *a ridge; a mark.*

māde̸, māi̯d.—*The* —— *milked the cows and* —— *the butter.*
sāle̸, sāi̯l.—*The house is for* ——. *The ships* ——.

SPELLER. 67

Lesson 153.

When the accent of a word ending in a single consonant preceded by a single vowel falls on any other syllable than the last, the final consonant is not doubled upon adding a termination beginning with a vowel.

bär'rel̥ed   kĭd'năp er   grŏv'el ing
ċăn'ċcl̥ed   jew'el er   chăn'nel ing
eăv'il̥ed   lī'bel er   coun'sel ing
ear'ol̥ed   mŏd'el er   mär'shal ing
chĭṣ'el̥ed   quar'rel er   pĕn'çil ing
ē'qual̥ed   rĕv'el er   shrĭv'el ing
grăv'el̥ed   trăv'el er   shŏv'el ing
găm'bol̥ed   wōr'ship er   pär'çel ing
lā'bel̥ed   vĭet'ual er   trăm'mel ing

Lesson 154.

PARTS OF THE HUMAN BODY.

eyes	head	bones	loins	joints
jaws	skin	knees	limbs	brains
lips	hair	heels	wrist	cheeks
ribs	face	soles	flesh	thighs
legs	hand	palms	beard	throat
toes	fist	nails	crown	breast
ears	chin	teeth	scalp	thumbs
nose	feet	lungs	skull	spleen
neck	arms	veins	mouth	tongue

The **spleen** is a spongy gland above the kidney, supposed by the ancients to be the seat of anger and ill-humored melancholy; hence the word also means *anger* or *ill humor*.

Lesson 155.

The plurals of most words are formed by adding *s* to the singular.

lŏfts	drēȧms	mī'ṣerṣ	rĭv'erṣ
wŏȩṣ	skātȩs	brī'erṣ	ôr'ḡanṣ
claẇṣ	clōvȩṣ	ġī'ants	jū'rorṣ
plēȧṣ	plȧ̇inṣ	rī'valṣ	mŏn'ȩ̇ẏṣ

Nouns ending with *ch* (*soft*), *sh*, *x*, *z*, or *s*, add *-es* to form the plural.

fŏx'eṣ	bĕnch'eṣ	drĕsṣ'eṣ	răd'ish eṣ
ärch'eṣ	mătch'cṣ	ḡlăsṣ'eṣ	bu̧l'rush eṣ
lỹṇx'eṣ	blŭsh'eṣ	cross'eṣ	wĭt'nesṣ eṣ
ĭnch'eṣ	skĕtch'cṣ	pēảch'eṣ	ĭsth'mus eṣ

Lesson 156.

fȧ̇int, *weak; languid.*	hȧ̇il, *frozen rain.*
fe̦int, *a pretense.*	hāle̸, *strong; healthy.*
fāte̸, *decree; lot.*	lȧ̇id, *participle of* lay.
fe̦te̸, *a festival.*	lāde̸, *to load; to dip.*
ḡȧ̇it, *manner of walking.*	lȧ̇in, *participle of* lie.
ḡāte̸, *an entrance.*	lāne̸, *a narrow road.*
ḡrāte̸, *a fire-place.*	bāse̸, *low; mean.*
ḡre̦āt, *large; grand.*	bāsṣ, *a part in music.*

Lay has for its preterit **laid**, and **lie** has **lay**: as, He told me to **lay** it down, and I *laid* it down; or, He told me to **lie** down, and I *lay* down. The ship **lay** (not *laid*) at anchor. They had **lain** (not *laid*) down on the grass. The book **lay** on the shelf.

Lesson 157.

Nouns ending in *f, ff,* and *fe* in most cases form their plurals regularly. Wharf has two plurals: *whurfs, wharves.*

pŭffs	rēefs	seärfs	be lḯefs'
mŭffs	g̃ŭlfs	stŭffs	re bŭffs'
eŭffs	wāi̯fs	prōōfs	mĭs'chi̯efs

Exceptions to the above rule; as *elf,* elves.

ĕlve̱s	sĕlve̱s	lōa̱ve̱s	shĕlve̱s
līve̱s	k̇nīve̱s	wolve̱s	thi̯ēve̱s
wīve̱s	ea̱l̇ve̱s	bēe̯ve̱s	our sĕlve̱s'
lēa̱ve̱s	hăl̇ve̱s	shēa̱ve̱s	yøur sĕlve̱s'

Lesson 158.

WORDS PERTAINING TO COLOR, AND SHADES OF COLOR.

jĕt	ĕb'on	rŭd'dy	pûr'ple̱
tĭnt	rṳ'by	sănd'y	săl'lōw̌
g̃rāy̌	ĭnk'y	sŏr'rel	dăp'ple̱d
drăb	sā'ble̱	blū'ish	seär'let
rōa̱n	ŏl'īve̱	rŭs'set	erĭm'sø̱n
fâi̯r	ăz'ure̱	yĕl'lōw̌	eär'mīne̱
pĭnk	ăm'ber	mŏt'le̱y	vẽr'dant
g̃rēe̱n	blŏnde̱	g̃ōld'e̱n	swạrth'y
brown	taw̌'ny	aụ'burn	vī'o lĕt

The deepest *black* is jet-black. A tint is a slight coloring distinct from the main color; as, red with a blue *tint.* Gray was formerly also spelled *grey;* that form is now used only in *greyhound,* from Icelandic *grey,* a dog. Azure is pronounced äzh'ur.

Lesson 159.

In these words the plurals are formed irregularly, and the plurals are to be found in the dictation exercises.

ŏx	He yoked the ŏx'en.
măn	Many mĕn of many minds.
chīld	The family had six chĭl'dren.
gōōse	The gēese swam in the pond.
mouse	The mīce gnawed the papers.
louse	Old hens often have līce.
fŏŏt	A yard measures three fēet.
tōōth	An adult has thirty-two tēeth.
wọm'an	Six wom'en sat in the coach.
pĕn'ny	Twelve pence make one shilling.

Lesson 160.

The following words are used chiefly in the plural.

ōats	ăsh'es	măt'ins	tī'dings
tŏngs	wā'ges	bĭt'ters	snŭff'ers
drĕgs	ăn'nals	bĕl'lŏws	trou'sers
gŏŏds	rĭch'es	mēa'sles	bĭll'iards
mēans	ăs'sets	vĕs'pers	scĭs'sors
dŭmps	mŏr'als	draw'ers	twēe'zers
	nĭp'pers	pĭnch'ers	

Webster says the spelling of **pinchers** is much to be preferred to *pincers*. The word **bellows** (bĕl'lus) is both singular and plural. **Vesper**, in its singular form, means pertaining to the evening, or to the service of *vespers*; **matin** pertains to the morning.

Lesson 161.

Most words ending in **o** form their plurals by adding **-es** to the singular. The following words end in *es*.

hē'rōęs   ear'gōęs   po tā'tōęs
ĉeh'ōęs   grŏt'tōęs   to mā'tōęs
nē'grōęs   eăl'i eōęs   tor nā'dōęs

When the final *o* is preceded by a consonant, the formation of the plural varies. The following words end in *s*.

hä'lōs   eăn'tōs   so prä'nōs
sō'lōs   lăs'sōs   ŏe tā'vōs
zē'rōs   quar'tōs   dŏm'i nōs
tȳ'rōs   pro vī'sōs   me měn'tōs

Lesson 162.

Require the pupil to fill the blanks below correctly.

bēąch, *a shore; a strand.* | nęęd, *want; necessity.*
bēęch, *a kind of tree.* | lęąf, *part of a plant.*
bēąt, *to strike; conquer.* | lįef, *willingly; gladly.*
bēęt, *a garden vegetable.* | męąn, *base; humble.*
flēą, *a small insect.* | mįen, *manner; bearing.*
flēę, *to run away.* | pęąçę, *quietness; calm.*
ķnēąd, *to work dough.* | pįeçę, *a part; a share.*

pęęl, pęąl.—*A* —— *of bells. An orange* ——.
hērę, hęąr.—*Sit thou* —— *and* —— *the speech.*
hēęl, hęąl.—*His wound in the* —— *will* ——.

Lesson 163.

Some words in the singular form are used in both numbers.

dēĕr   *Twenty* dēĕr *were in the park.*
shēĕp *The* shēĕp *were all shorn.*
swīnĕ *A* swīnĕ *is also called a hog.*

Words ending in *y*, preceded by a consonant, change *y* into *i* and add *es* to form the plural.

bĕr'riĕṣ	¢oun'tiĕṣ	ā'ġen çiĕṣ
¢ăn'diĕṣ	chĕr'riĕṣ	ḡrō'çer iĕṣ
stō'riĕṣ	pĕn'niĕṣ	rĕm'e diĕṣ

Penny has two plurals: *pennies* denotes the number of coins; *pence*, the amount of pennies in value. An English penny is worth about two cents, or four farthings.

Lesson 164.

PROPERTIES AND RELATIONS OF LIQUIDS.

flōw̸	ōōzĕ	dăṉk	quàff	flŏŏd
drĭp	skĭm	dămp	frŏth	stēạm
shĕd	sōạk	rēĕk	moist	spûrt
fōạm	lāvĕ	hàzĕ	stēĕp	squīrt
drŏp	wạsh	swĭm	spout	frēĕzĕ
ḡŭsh	fūmĕ	seŭm	dousĕ	drĕnch

Rivers **flow** to the sea; water **drips** from the eaves; tears and blood are **shed**; the pond **freezes** over; the meadows **reek** with vapor; fountains **gush**; the sea **foams**; blood **spouts** from a vein; and the low grounds are **flooded** by the deluge.

SPELLER. 73

Lesson 165.

When the singular ends in *y* preceded by a vowel, the plural is formed by adding *s*.

ăl'lĕȳs văl'lĕȳs tûr'kĕȳs jŏĕk'ĕȳs
ăb'bĕȳs vŏl'lĕȳs mĕd'lĕȳs lăĕk'ĕȳs
ĕs'sayś fo rāyś pär'lĕȳs vīçĕ'royś
ĕn'voyś pul'lĕȳs monk'ĕȳs jŏûr'nĕȳs

An **abbey** is a house used for religious purposes. A **medley** is a confused mass, a mixture. An **envoy** is one dispatched on an errand or a mission; a **viceroy** one who rules in the name of the king. A **foray** is a sudden incursion in a border war, and a **parley** is usually a conference between enemies. A **volley** is a flight of shot. **Essay** is pronounced ĕs'sa; **assay**, as sā'.

Lesson 166.

TITLES, AND THEIR ABBREVIATIONS.

Mā'jor,	*Maj.*	Căp'tăin,	*Capt.*
Dŏe'tor,	*Dr.*	Mĭs'tresś,	*Mrs.*
Mĭs'ter,	*Mr.*	Es quīrĕ',	*Esq.*
Bĭsh'op,	*Bp.*	Colŏ'nel (kûr'-),	*Col.*
Dĕa'con,	*Dea.*	Ġĕn'er al,	*Gen.*
Căsh ı̌er,'	*Cash.*	Rĕv'er end,	*Rev.*

Reading Exercise.—She sells sea-shells. Gaze on the gay gray brigade. The sea ceaseth and it sufficeth us. A cup of coffee in a copper coffee-cup. Say, should such a shapely sash shabby stitches show? Strange strategic statistics. Shovel soft snow slowly.

Lesson 167.

Derivatives formed from words ending in a double consonant, in adding syllables, commonly retain both consonants.

ĕbḅĕd	ŏdd'ly	skĭll'fụl nesṣ
ērrĕd	stĭff'ly	wĭll'fụl nesṣ
bŭzẓĕd	ḡrŭff'ly	blĭss'fụl nesṣ
pŭffĕd	ḡrōss'ly	ḡlàss'i nesṣ
pàssĕd	fụll'ness	màss'ĭvĕ ly
hĭssĕd	dŭll'ness	en rōll'ment
stŭffĕd	drĕss'ing	en ḡrōss'ment
erŏssĕd	thrạll'dŏm	in stạll'ment

Lesson 168.

Form sentences from the following words.

mĕạt, *flesh; food.*
mēĕt, *to come together.*
mētĕ, *to measure.*
pēĕr, *an equal.*
pīēr, *solid stone-work.*
rĕạd, *to peruse.*
rēĕd, *a hollow plant.*
sĕạ, *a body of water.*
sēĕ, *to behold.*

sēạl, *a stamp; animal.*
sēĕl, *to render blind.*
çĕịl, *to overlay a room.*
sēạṣ, *plural of* sea.
sēĕṣ, *beholds.*
sēịzĕ, *to lay hold of.*
sēạr, *to burn; wither.*
sēĕr, *a prophet.*
çērĕ, *to cover with wax.*

sēạm, sēĕm.—*We sew a* ———. *To* ——— *is to appear.*
sēĕd, çēdĕ.—*We sow* ———. *To* ——— *is to give up.*

Lesson 169.

Monosyllables ending with the sound of **k**, in which *c* follows the vowel, usually add the letter *k*. This is also done with the accented syllable of some dissyllables, and sometimes also to avoid the soft sound of *c*. The *k* is now omitted at the end of most words of more than one syllable.

spĕ¢k	frĕ¢k'l¢	rŏl'li¢k¢d	tón'ic
bri¢k	thi¢k'et	trăf'fi¢k¢d	tŏp'ie
shŏ¢k	stŏ¢k'ing	frŏl'i¢k¢d	eū'bie
plŭ¢k	tri¢k'l¢	mĭm'i¢k¢d	pŭb'lie

Exceptions to the above rules.

tăle	zine	băr'ra¢k	hill'o¢k
fīse	pie'nic	hŭm'mo¢k	hăm'mo¢k

Lesson 170.

DAYS AND MONTHS, AND THEIR ABBREVIATIONS.

Sŭn'day,	*Sun.*	März,	*Mar.*
Mŏn'dạў,	*Mon.*	Ā'pril,	*Apr.*
Tūȩs'dạў,	*Tues.*	Ju lȳ',	*Jul.*
Wĕ₫nȩs'dạў,	*Wed.*	Aụ'ğust,	*Aug.*
Thûrs'day,	*Thurs.*	Sep tĕm'ber,	*Sept.*
Frī'day,	*Fri.*	Oc tō'ber,	*Oct.*
Săt'ur day,	*Sat.*	No vĕm'ber,	*Nov.*
Jăn'ū a ry,	*Jan.*	De çĕm'ber,	*Dec.*
Fĕb'ru a ry,	*Feb.*	Ȼḫrisṭ'mas,	*Xmas.*

May and June are usually written in full; the seasons, Sprīng, Sūm'mer, Aụ'tumṇ and Wĭn'ter, are also not abbreviated.

Lesson 171.

In derivatives formed from words ending with a silent **e**, the *e* is generally retained when the termination begins with a consonant.

pāle̸'ness̸	fīne̸'ness̸	in çīte̸'ment
hāte̸'ful	ḡāme̸'ster	ma tūre̸'ly
chāste̸'ly	flĕd̸g̸e̸'ling	con çīse̸'ness̸
mo̤ve̸'ment	stärve̸'ling	de fāçe̸'ment

Some exceptions to the above rule.

wi̸s̸dŏm	jŭd̸g̸'ment	nûrs'ling
w̸hōl'ly	lŏd̸g̸'ment	a brĭd̸g̸'ment

Lesson 172.

SYNONYMOUS ADJECTIVES.

nȧs'ty	fĭlth'y	squa̤l'id	im pūre̸'
na̤u̸g̸h̸t'y	per vẽrse̸'	cor rŭpt'	sĭn'ful
ob seūre̸'	ḡlōōm'y	dŭsk'y	shăd'ed
oc cŭlt'	hĭd'den	sē'cret	un knōw̸n'
pa̤l'try	lĭt'tle̸	pĕt'ty	trī'fling
pēa̸çe̸'ful	un mo̤ve̸d'	plăç'id	se rēne̸'
pẽr'fect	hō'ly	blāme̸'less̸	fa̤u̸lt'less̸
pĭth'y	con çīse̸'	com păct'	point'ed
pēe̸v'ish	frĕt'ful	chûrl'ish	crŭst'y

Nasty, applied in England also to the weather, is a Scandinavian word; **filthy** is English; **squalid** is Latin; and **impure,** Latin through the French. **Concise** is pronounced kon çīçe̸'.

Lesson 173.

Derivatives formed from words ending in silent e, when the termination begins with a vowel, generally omit the e.

ūṣ'aġe̶ ġu̶īd'ançe̶ fōrç'i ble̶
dūr'ançe̶ plūm'aġe̶ sāl'a ble̶
flēe̶'çy ġri̶ēv'ançe̶ mov'a ble̶

Exceptions to the above rule.

dȳe̶'ing tŏe̶'ing pēa̶çe̶'a ble̶
tĭnġe̶'ing hŏe̶'ing chärġe̶'a ble̶
sĭnġe̶'ing sho̶e̶'ing chānġe̶'a ble̶

Dyeing, the act of coloring, is so spelled to prevent confusion with *dying*, pertaining to death.

Lesson 174.

bȳ, *near at hand.*
bu̶ȳ, *to purchase.*
clīme̶, *region; climate.*
climb̶, *to mount up.*
die̶, *to cease to live.*
dȳe̶, *to color; to stain.*
iṣle̶, *a small island.*
aiṣle̶, *a narrow passage.*

migh̶t, *power; ability.*
mite̶, *a small particle.*
nigh̶t, *darkness.*
kn̶igh̶t, *title of honor.*
size̶, *bulk; extent.*
sigh̶s, *plural of* sigh.
rȳe̶, *a kind of grain.*
w̶rȳ, *crooked; twisted.*

lie̶, lȳe̶.—*Do not* —— *down.* —— *is used in making soap. A* —— *is a falsehood.*
quire̶, choīr.—*A* —— *of paper. The* —— *sang a hymn. How many sheets are in a* ——?

Lesson 175.

Words ending in -er.

nī'ter	sā'ber	çĕn'ter	spĕe'ter
fī'ber	ō'e̸ḱer	sŏm'ber	eăl'i ber
mē'ter	ŭm'ber	mēa̸'ḡer	thē'a ter
mī'ter	lŭs'ter	s̸ćep'ter	ma ne̸ū'ver

Exceptions to the above.

| ā'er̸ǵ | ō'ḡr̸ǵ | lū'er̸ǵ | măs'sa er̸ǵ |

Niter is also called *saltpeter*. A **fiber** is a thread-like substance. A **miter** is a bishop's head-dress. **Ocher** is a fine clay, commonly yellow; **umber** is a brown ocher. An **ogre** is a monster in fairy tales, and a **specter** is a ghost. **Lucre** signifies gain, profit.

Lesson 176.

WORDS PERTAINING TO TIME.

ēv̸é	sōōn	ĕv'er	mŏd'ern
āy̸é	dāte̸	àft'er	nŏv'ĭçe̸
āḡe̸	lāte̸	nĕv'er	mŏr'rōẃ
dāy̸	yōre̸	ēa̸r'ly	rē'çent
now	frĕsh	prī'or	lāte̸'ly
thĕn	y̸óŭng	to-dāy'	al'wāy's
whĕn	sĭnçe̸	ōld'er	sēa̸'sóń
tĭlÝ	whīle̸	jūn'ior	mō'ment
nōōn	a nŏn'	sēn'ior	fôrt'nīgh́t

Aye, meaning *always*, is pronounced ā; as an affirmative vote, pronounced ī. **Yore** means in long time past.

Lesson 177.

Words ending in -ise; in the following *s* is pronounced like *z*.

ad vīṣé′	com prīṣé′	çīr′eum çīṣé
de vīṣé′	sur prīṣé′	af frăn′chīṣé
re vīṣé′	dis g̃uīṣé′	eŏm′pro mīṣé
de mīṣé′	chas tīṣé′	erīt′i çīṣé
ex çīṣé′	frăn′chīṣé	dis frăn′chīṣé
ap prīṣé′	ĕx′er çīṣé	en frăn′chīṣé
sur mīṣé′	ĕx′or çīṣé	ĕn′ter prīṣé
pre mīṣé′	ăd ver tīṣé′	sū per vīṣé′
de spīṣé′	eăt′e ehīṣé	mēr′chan dīṣé

The above, chiefly verbs, are the principal words in the English language ending in ise; in çīṣé″, to cut in, might be added. Exercise, to set in action, is pronounced nearly like exorcise, to cast out spirits, although in the latter the *o* is sounded slightly.

Lesson 178.

Fill the blanks below, and form the other words into sentences.

bōẃl, *a concave vessel.*
bōlÝ, *pod of a plant.*
bōlé, *body of a tree.*
g̃rōắn, *a moaning sound.*
g̃rōẃn, *increased.*
hōlé, *a hollow place.*
ẃhōlé, *all; entire.*

mōắt, *a ditch; a trench.*
mōté, *a small particle.*
ōắr, *a long paddle.*
ō′ér, *contraction of* over.
ōré, *unrefined metal.*
pōlé, *a rod; a long stick.*
pōlÝ, *the head.*

nō, Ḱnōẃ.—*Did you* —— *him?* ——, *I did not.*
pōúr, pōré.—*The sweat did* —— *from every* ——.

Lesson 179.

COMMON ABBREVIATIONS.

East,	E.	Last month,	Ult.
West,	W.	This month,	Inst.
North,	N.	Next month,	Prox.
South,	S.	Ex am'ple,	Ex.
Num'ber,	No.	Man'u script,	MS.
An'swer,	Ans.	Aft'er noon,	P. M.
Coun'ty,	Co.	Gŏv'ern or,	Gov.
Fōre'noon,	A. M.	Gĕn'tle men,	Messrs.
Vŏl'ume,	Vol.	Hŏn'or a ble,	Hon.
Rāil'rōad,	R. R.	Pro fĕss'or,	Prof.
Pōst'script,	P. S.	Pōst Of'fice,	P. O.
Mount'ain,	Mt.	Tāke nō'tice,	N. B.

Lesson 180.

Fill the blanks below, and compose other sentences.

muse, *to meditate.*
mews, *an inclosure.*
slue, *to turn aside.*
slew, *did slay; killed.*
flue, *passage for smoke.*
flew, *did fly.*

hue, *color; tint.*
hew, *to cut; to chop.*
Hugh, *a man's name.*
yew, *an evergreen tree.*
ewe, *a female sheep.*
you, *person spoken to.*

blew, blue.—The wind —— gently over the dark —— sea. The color of the clear sky is ——.
due, dew.—The note is ——. The —— is falling.

SPELLER. 81

Lesson 181.

Words spelled alike, but pronounced differently.

Aṷ'g̅ust, *eighth month.*
aṷ g̅ŭst', *grand; awful.*
eŏm'păet, *an agreement.*
com păet', *firm; solid.*
eŏn'sôrt, *a companion.*
eon sôrt', *to associate.*
eŏn'viet, *a criminal.*
eon vĭet', *to prove guilty.*

g̅ăl'lant, *brave.*
g̅al lănt', *a beau.*
ĭm'press, *mark; stamp.*
im prĕss', *to stamp.*
mĭn'ute (-it), 60 *seconds.*
mĭ nūte', *very small.*
prŏd'ūçe, *that yielded.*
pro dūçe', *to bring forth.*

rebel.—*A —— is one who ——s.* frequent.—*His visits were ——. To —— is to visit often.*

Lesson 182.

The following words, similar to the above, are *nouns* when accented on the first syllable, and *verbs* when accented on the last. Let the pupils place the proper accent and marks upon them in both relations, and define them.

af fix	eon test	eon sole	pro ject
ae çent	eon trast	ex port	pro test
eom press	con vert	fer ment	sub ject
eon çert	con verse	im port	ree ord
eon duet	des ert	in çense	sur vey
eon fliet	di g̅est	ob ject	tor ment

An **affix** is a syllable joined to the end of a word; to **affix** means to join at the end. **Incense** is the odor of spices and gums burned in religious rites; to **incense** is to enrage.

P. S. B.—6.

Lesson 183.

The **su** and **si** in these words are sounded like *zh*.

vĭṣ'ion	dĭ vĭṣ'ion	ex elū'ṣion
mĕa̸ṣ'ūr̸e	de çĭṣ'ion	ex plō'ṣion
trĕa̸ṣ'ūr̸e	ad hē'ṣion	eol lĭṣ'ion
plĕa̸ṣ'ūr̸e	de lū'ṣion	eom pōṣ'ūr̸e
ūṣ'ū al	in vā'ṣion	in elōṣ'ūr̸e
ū'ṣū ry	eon elū'ṣion	dis elōṣ'ūr̸e

The books which help you most are those which make you think most. The hardest way of learning is by easy reading; but a great book that comes from a great thinker,—it is a ship of thought, deep freighted with truth and with beauty.

Lesson 184.

Fill the blanks below with the proper words.

dăm, *to stop the flow.*
dămn̸, *to condemn.*
drăm, *a drink of liquor.*
drăc̸h̸m, *60 grains.*
jăm, *a conserve of fruit.*
jămb̸, *part of a chimney.*
lăc̸ks, *wants; needs.*

lăx, *loose.*
lăps, *plural of* lap.
lăpse̸, *to fall.*
răc̸k, *to stretch.*
w̸răc̸k, *a sea-plant.*
răp, *to strike.*
w̸răp, *to fold together.*

to, tōō, tw̸o.—*He was —— late —— see the apple cut in ——. —— be, or not —— be.*

To is pronounced **to̤** when emphasized, or standing alone, but **to̅o̅** when not emphatic. **Too** and **two** have always the long sound.

SPELLER. 83

Lesson 185.

Words derived from the Greek, having the sound of *i* in the first syllable, are generally spelled with a *y*.

tўp'ie	sўm'pa thy	tўr'an ny
çўn'ie	sўl'la blǿ	sўm'me try
phўş'ies	pўr'a mĭd	hўs tĕr'ie
hўm'nal	sўn'o nўm	çўl'in der
sўr'ingǿ	syn ŏp'sis	mўs'te ry
hў'men	dў'nas ty	dў năm'ie
hў'drȧ	hў'dro ġen	hў'a çĭnth

Typic means of the nature of a *type*; **cynic**, having the qualities of a surly dog; a **hymnal** is a book of hymns; and **physics** is the science of nature.

Lesson 186.

WORDS PERTAINING TO DISEASE, MEDICINES, ETC.

ĭlÿ	seärş	sprāi̧n	ĭlÿ'nesş	pow'derş
stў	pāi̧nş	hĕalth	môr'bid	ăb'sǿĕsş
wĕn	pĭlłş	fĕl'on	un wĕlł'	plȧs'ter
sōrǿ	wǿund	fē'ver	tў'phus	diş ēaşǿ'
bānǿ	boilş	vī'rus	at tăçk'	ai̧l'ment
ġout	spăşmş	tū'mor	in fēet'	ea tärɤḩ'
fīts	ā'ġūǿ	vĕn'om	pŭst'ūlǿ	hĕad'āeḩǿ
drŭġ	säłvǿ	pal'şy	drŏp'sy	pōṇl'tiçǿ
eōld	quăçk	ŭl'çer	poi'şǿn	tў'phoid

Which words in the above are the names of *diseases*? Which indicate *outward applications*? Which refer to *effects of injuries*?

Lesson 187.

Note carefully the spelling of these words.

pûr	ḡu̶ärd	văs'sal	pŏs tīl'ion
pẽrt	lŏd̶ġe̶	tăs'sel	dŏl'or øŭs
vi̶ew	mẽrġe̶	vīr'ġin	sŏv'er e̶iġn
sure̶	swĕa̶t	tûr'ġid	ăm a te̶ur'
sho̶e̶	tīg̶h̶t	mȳr'tle̶	prŏs'e lȳte̶
lewd	truçe̶	sẽr'aph	sĕp'a rāte̶
ḵnŏb	ḡu̶īde̶	păl'açe̶	sē'ere çy
jōy̶l	w̶rŏng	mŏn̠'ġer	ĕe'sta sy
ea̶rl	cōrp̶s̶	sĕn'ate̶	ŏs'çil lāte̶
sīg̶n	tĕmp̶t	tōy̶'ard	be ḡin'ning

Lesson 188.

bĕll̶, *a sounding vessel.*
bĕll̶e̶, *a fine lady.*
brĕa̶d, *a kind of food.*
brĕd, *trained.*
çĕll̶, *a small room.*
sĕll̶, *to dispose of.*
çĕnt, *a small coin.*
se̶ĕnt, *a perfume.*
sĕnt, *did send.*
sẽrf, *a slave.*
sûrf, *broken waves.*

sĕn'sor, *a kind of nerve.*
çĕns'er, *vase for incense.*
çĕn'sor, *a harsh critic.*
ḡu̶ĕst, *a visitor.*
ḡu̶ĕss̶e̶d, *did guess.*
çĕl'lar, *an under-room.*
sĕll̶'er, *one who sells.*
rĕst, *to repose.*
w̶rĕst, *to take by force.*
sẽrġe̶, *a twilled stuff.*
sûrġe̶, *a large wave.*

lĕd, lĕa̶d.—*He* —— *him astray.* —— *is a metal.*
rĕd, rĕa̶d.—*He* —— *the book.* —— *is a color.*

SPELLER 85

Lesson 189.

Words liable to be misspelled.

phāṣe̸	sā'tyr	çīr'eu̸it	se̸ī ăt'ie
rōḡu̸e̸	sĭb'yl	eûr'tai̸n	ăd'di ble̸
sau̸çe̸	e̸ȳ'ing	jĕøp'ard	stū'pe fȳ
thrall̸	vĭg̈'il	môr'tĭse̸	vĭt'ri fȳ
sōu̸rçe̸	tĕn'or	fôr'fe̸it	vĭt're ø̸ŭs
slūi̸çe̸	tăl'on	eŏl'leg̈e̸	dŏm'i çĭle̸
ẏrīthe̸	răb'id	p̸sal'ter	sū per sēde̸'
he̸īg̈ḵt	lĭ'bel	jøûr'ne̸y	văç'il lāte̸
plīg̈ḵt	hū'mor	sûr'fe̸it	fäs'çi nāte̸
ple̸d̸g̈e̸	mam mä'	g̃äl'lo̸w̸s	eŏl on nāde̸'
hēa̸rse̸	rĕv'el	jĕa̸l'ø̸ŭs	be lēa̸'g̈u̸er

Lesson 190.

COMMERCIAL TERMS AND ABBREVIATIONS.

to̤, or ăt,	a or @	hŭn'dred-we̤ig̈ḵt,	cwt.
băr'rel,	Bbl.	dĭt'to (the same),	Do.
dĕb̸t'or,	Dr.	re çe̤i̸ve̸d',	rec'd.
băl'ançe̸,	bal.	pāy̸'ment,	pay't.
eŏm'pa ny,	Co.	pĕn'ny we̤ig̈ḵt,	pwt.
a mount',	amt.	ĭn'ter est,	int.
ae eount',	acct.	dĭs'eount,	dis.
eăsh (or eol lĕet')		mēr'chan dīṣe̸,	mdse.
ŏn de lĭv'er y,	C.O.D.	erĕd'it or,	Cr.

Do not wait for extraordinary opportunities for great actions, but make use of common situations.

Lesson 191.

Words which require care in spelling.

vāḡu̶e̶	ō'dor	chăp'el	săt'el līte̶
ḡōu̶rd	pa pä'	trĭp'le̶	flăg'e̶o lĕt
sw̶ōrd	ăr'id	hĕi̶f'er	wōol'li ness̶
vĕrġe̶	lĭl'y	prĭm'er	sĭb'yl līne̶
pûrġe̶	eŏp'y	nĭe̶k'el	săe'eḵa rīne̶
bu̶ĭld	du ĕt'	pĭġ'e̶ŏn	rĕn'dez̶ vou̶s̶
w̶räth	săl'ad	elăm'or	hĕm'or rḵaġe̶
w̶rôth	tĕn'on	wĕe̶'vi̶l	erȳs'tal līne̶
p̶shaw̶	la pĕl'	ere çhe̶t̶'	sŏph'o mōre̶
p̶säi̶m	e̶ī'der	eŏn'du̶it	săe'ri leġe̶

It is better to know much of a few things than a little of many things.

Lesson 192.

WORDS REFERRING TO SHAPE OR FORM.

bōw̶	ärch	thĭe̶k	ō'val	.lĕngth
bĕnt	slĭm	erōok	ē've̶n	sphĕre̶
lŏng	lŭmp	point	tā'per	brĕadth
wĭde̶	shôrt	bŭlġe̶	e rĕet'	năr'rōw̶
lēa̶n	stout	round	lĕv'el	eŏn'vex
ta̤lY̶	brø̶ad	slànt	bŭlk'y	eŏn'eāve̶

A ball or sphere is ——. When an object is hollow and curved, we say it is ——; when it is rising or swelling into rounded form, we say it is ——; when shaped like an egg, it is ——.

GENERAL REVIEW OF PART II.

Lesson 193.

Repeat the rule given in Lesson 150.

blĕss̸	drĭll̸	sta̤ll̸	hŭff̸
brȧss̸	dwĕll̸	quĕll̸	mĭff̸
chĕss̸	frĭll̸	quĭll̸	mŭff̸
ḡlŏss̸	k̸nĕll̸	sc̶ŭll̸	rŭff̸
c̶rŏss̸	k̸nōll̸	thrĭll̸	mŭss̸

Lesson 194.

Repeat the rule given in Lesson 151.

ĭnn̸′ing	a bŭt′tal	ab hŏr′rençe̸
k̸nĭt′ting	ac̶ quĭt′tal	re mĭt′tançe̸
slĕd′ding	es tŏp′pel	oc̶ c̶ŭr′rençe̸
spĭn′ning	pro pĕl′ler	ad mĭt′tançe̸
whĭp′ping	c̶on trōl′ler	re bĕll̸′io̸ŭs

Lesson 195.

Repeat the rule given in Lesson 153.

ĕd′it or	c̶ăn′on īze̸	hĭn′der ançe̸
a̤u̸′di tor	c̶ăn non āde̸′	dĭf′fer ençe̸
c̶ŭs′tom er	ôr′phan aġe̸	sŭf′fer ançe̸
lĭst̸′e̸n er	mĕş′mer ĭşm	c̶ŏn′fer ençe̸
rĕf er ēe̸′	c̶ŏm′bat ant	tĕm′per ançe̸

REVIEW. (Continued.)

Lesson 196.

Repeat the rules given in Lesson 155.

ŏs'trich es	skĭr'mish es	ădz'es
sănd'wich es	vär'nish es	chĭntz'es
dis pătch'es	păr'a dŏx es	eär'eass̸ es
blĕm'ish es	eru̧'ci fīx es	măt'tress̸ es

Repeat the rules given in Lesson 161.

bŭf'fa lō¢s	măn i fĕs'tō¢s	nŭn'ci ōs
vī rā'ḡō¢s	dĕs per ā'dō¢s	stī lĕt'tōs
vol eā'nō¢s	se răḡl'iōs	pal mĕt'tōs
mos qu̧ī'tō¢s	vīr tu ō'sōs	pōrt fōl'iōs

Lesson 197.

Repeat the rule given in Lesson 165.

joys	de eoys'	re lāy's'	sûr'vey's
ḡu̧ys	af frāy's'	de lāy's'	nōs¢'ḡāy's
drāy's	dis plāy's'	al loys'	hŏl'i dāy's
buo̧y̆s	Sē'poys	eŏn'voys	eôr'du roys

Repeat the rule given in Lesson 163.

ḡū'lo ġi̇es	cĕm'e tĕr i̇es	de fī'cien çies
pŏl'i çies	sĕm'i na ri̇es	au̧ṯx̱ īl'ia ri̇es
ḡăl'ler i̇es	dis tĭll'er i̇es	ne çĕs'si ti̇es
eăl'um ni̇es	hos tĭl'i ti̇es	de līṉ'quen çies

SPELLER. 89

REVIEW. (Continued.)

Lesson 198.

Repeat the rule given in Lesson 167.

kĭss'ing	ŏdd'i ty	as sĕss'a blę
păss'ing	drōll'er y	sue çĕss'ful ly
seŏff'ing	nŭl'li fȳ	pro fĕss'ed ly
snĭff'ing	elăs'si fȳ	ğŭl li bĭl'ĭ ty
dwĕll'ing	dis mĭss'al	er rō'ne ǫŭs
quĕll'ing	trĕs'pass er	con ḡrĕs'sion al
small'ness	trans ḡress'or	em băr'rass ment
blŭff'ness	en fęǫff'ment	dĭs til lā'tion
tĭll'age	im prĕss'ment	in stạl lā'tion
ŏff'spring	in thrạll'ment	ĭn stil lā'tion

Lesson 199.

Repeat the rule given in Lesson 169.

trăck	răck'et	ęḱa ŏt'ie
chĕck	ẃrĕck'age	eḱŏl'er ie
elĭck	ḱnŭck'lę	ee çĕn'trie
ḱnŏck	eŏl'ick y	em phăt'ie
trŭck	ğär'lick y	ē niğ măt'ie
eăck'lę	pḱtḱĭs'ick y	ĕn er ğĕt'ie
eŏck'lę	hăv'ock ing	ee elē și ăs'tie
chŭck'lę	bĭv'ouăcked	en thū și ăst'ie

Exceptions to the Rule.

răn'sack	bụll'ock	eăs'sock	păd'dock

REVIEW. (Continued.)

Lesson 200.

Repeat the rule given in Lesson 171.

ĭm'aġe̸ ry	blīthe̸'some̸	ꞓom plēte̸'ness̸
en tīre̸'ty	a bāte̸'ment	sō'cia ble̸ ness̸
se vēre̸'ly	al lūre̸'ment	sĕp'a rate̸ ly
ăd'vērse̸ ly	be ġᴜ̸īle̸'ment	de çī'sīve̸ ly
a ꞓūte̸'ness̸	be rēᶏve̸'ment	en ꞓøūr'aġe̸ ment
e lōpe̸'ment	in dôrse̸'ment	aḡ ḡrăn'dīze̸ ment
ef fāçe̸'ment	chăs'tise̸ ment	ad vēr'tise̸ ment

Exceptions to the Rule.

dū'ly tru̧'ly ĭn flam mā'tion aꞓ ꞣnŏẉl'edġ ment

Lesson 201.

Repeat the rule given in Lesson 173.

e rās̨'ūre̸	de s̨ir'øŭs	aḡ ḡri̧ēv'ançe̸
ex pōs̨'ūre̸	es pous̨'al	ad vī'so̧ ry
dĕf"i nīte̸	ex trēm'ist	ĭn'sti ġā tor
ꞓom pŏs̨'īte̸	be li̧ēv'ing	tĕl e seŏp'ie
de çei̧v'ing	ꞓo ēr'cion	çĭv'il ĭz ing
en ḡāg'ing	ꞓom mēr'cial	sŭb'si dīz ing
in ꞓrēᶏs'ing	ꞓon nīv'ançe̸	sy̆m'pa thīz ing

Exceptions to the Rule.

out rā'ġe̸øŭs sērv'içe̸ a ble̸ ăd van tā'ġe̸øŭs

REVIEW. (Continued.)

Words illustrating the foregoing rules.

Lesson 202.

tiff	bär′red	brăg′gart	prŏs′per ous
rȧff	bĕg′ged	drŭg′gist	răn′eor ous
gall	bit′ten	ex çĕl′ling	seȧn′dal īze
skill	bĭd′den	de tēr′ring	eŏn′su late
seroll	ĭn′ner	for bĭd′ding	ĭn′fer ençe
trill	sĭn′ner	fĕr′ret ing	măg′net işm
grill	jŏb′ber	găm′bol ing	văp′or īze
ĕress	shŭt′ter	eŏl′lar ing	sĭg′nal īze
flŏss	slĭp′per	rēa′şon ing	pēr′son age
gness	drŭm′mer	ĕn′ter ing	păt′ron age

Lesson 203.

bŏss′eş	săl′vōş	frāy′ş	răil′ler ies
elȧss′eş	frĕs′eōş	stāy′ş	rhȧp′so dies
bēech′eş	măn′gōş	eär′boyş	prŏph′e çies
brēach′eş	mŏt′tōes	bĕl′fries	shrŭb′ber ies
wrĕtch′eş	eȧm′e ōş	beau′ties	treaş′ūr ies
păr′ish eş	stū′di ous	chăr′i ties	ĭn′dus tries
flour′ish eş	pōr′ti eōes	eo quĕt′ries	jeȧl′ous ies
ĭn′dex eş	ĕm′bry ōş	dī′a ries	făl′la çies
vôr′tex eş	al bī′nōş	dȳ′nas ties	făn′ta sies
tō′paz eş	ea sī′nōş	lŭx′ū ries	făe′ul ties

REVIEW. (Continued.)

Words illustrating the foregoing rules.

Lesson 204.

snŭff'lø	ad dĭ'tion	crăȼk'lø
smĕl̄l'ing	re mĭs'sion	bĕȼk'øn
prĕss'ūrø	pro ḡrĕss'ĭvø	bŭȼk'ler
re bŭff'ing	pos sĕss'ĭvø	quĭȼk'øn
ap pal̄l'ing	fal lā'cĭøŭs	brăȼk'ish
ad drĕss'ing	doḡ măt'ie	e lăs'tie
chĭl̄l'i ness	cos̄ mĕt'ie	el lĭp'tie
mŏss'i ness	ḡī ḡăn'tie	ec stăt'ie
mȧs'sĭvø ness	in trĭn'sie	au thĕn'tie
ḡlŏss'i ness	bȧr băr'ie	pro phĕt'ie

Lesson 205.

ob tūsø'ness	lēi'surø ly	dŏm'i çīlø
ob seūrø'ness	sĕnsø'less ly	fals'i ty
ab strusø'ness	shāmø'ful ly	vēr'si fȳ
noi'sŏmø ness	līkø'li hōod	vĕnt'ūr øŭs
eȧrø'less ness	im provø'ment	vīrt'ū øŭs
lŏvø'li ness	ob s̄ērv'ançø	in quīr'y
ăe'eu ratø ly	pur sū'ançø	ef fū'sĭvø
ăd'e quātø ly	com păr'a tĭvø	trans lāt'or
ŏb'sti natø ly	com păr'i son	blas phĕm'ing
of fĕn'sĭvø ly	cŏm pe tĭ'tion	sup pōs̄'a blø

PART III.—ETYMOLOGY.

In this department will be found an explanation of many of the prefixes and suffixes employed in word-building, interspersed, as in the previous lessons, with language-lessons of various kinds.

Lesson 206.

PRIMITIVE AND DERIVATIVE WORDS.

Primitive words are those which are not derived from any other word in the language. The following are primitive words of the Anglo-Saxon or Middle English period (A. D. 1200-1500).

ăsk	rŏt	dōte̸	bāke̸	clŏth
coō	woō	fo͜lk	rĕa̸p	he̸ärth
mĭx	kĭn	lĭsp	soōt	shrewd
nĭp	ōẃn	păth	drēa̸m	frīghyt
gŭm	rĭd	spĭt	frēa̸k	thrĕa̸d

Derivative words formed from the above.

ăske̸d	soōt'y	dō'tage̸	drēa̸m'less̸
woōe̸d	gŭm'my	clōth'ing	frēa̸k'ish
mĭxe̸d	kĭn'ship	rĭd'dance̸	shrewd'ness̸
nĭppe̸d	ōẃn'er	fo͜lk'-lōre̸	thrĕa̸d'bâre̸
bāke̸d	rŏt'te̸n	păth'wāý	frīght'ful

In a language like ours, where so many words are derived from other languages, there are few modes of instruction more profitable than that of accustoming young people to seek for the etymology or primary meaning of the words they use.

Lesson 207.

Compound words are formed by uniting two simple words.

out′set	lănd′lôrd	dōōmş′dāý	kēy′-stōnḗ
hĕạd′lŏng	chär′ećọ̄ạl	nīgh́t′fạlḮ	dȳḗ′-stŭff́
ōạt′mēạl	mēạn′tīmḗ	hāíl′stōnḗ	wĕll′-mēạ́nt
nōōn′dāý	tōōth′-āeh́ḗ	quĭćk′sănd	wạtch′-wŏrd

wạ′ter-fạlḮ	lĕt′ter-bŏx	pōst′al-eärd
pow′der-flȧsk	thŭn′der-bōlt	mŭsk′-mĕl on
eŏp′y-bŏŏk	hănd́′ker chị̈ḗf	eămp′-mēḗt ing
hȯn′ḗȳ-ćōmb́	seh́ōōl′-mȧs ter	spĕll′ing-bŏŏk

Lesson 208.

bĭn, *a box for grain.*
been, *past particip. of* be.
çit, *a citizen.*
sĭt, *to rest on a seat.*
ḡĭlt, *overlaid with gold.*
ḡḯilt, *crịme; offense.*
hĭm, *objective case of* he.
hȳmń, *a sacred song.*

kĭll̇, *to put to death.*
kĭln̆, *an oven for drying.*
lĭmb́, *a branch; member.*
lĭmń, *to draw or paint.*
mĭst, *fog; fine rain.*
mĭssḗd, *past par. of* miss.
nĭt, *egg of an insect.*
ḱnĭt, *to unite closely.*

ĭn, ĭnń. — *He lodged at night —— the public ——.*
rĭng, ẃrĭng. — *We —— a bell, but we —— clothes
to force out water. A —— is a circle.*

⸺ Set, sit.—We say the sun has **set**, but human beings **sit**. A hen does not **set**—she **sits**; but we **set** a hen when we cause her to **sit** upon eggs.

Lesson 209.

SUFFIXES.

A **suffix** is a letter òr syllable added to the end of a word. In the following words **-er** and **-or** are suffixes, and signify *one who;* as **caller**, *one who* calls. In some words the suffixes **-ar** and **-ant** have the same meaning, as given below. From the words in the last column require the pupil to form words similar to those in the first three columns.

dĭḡ'ḡer	ăct'or	lī'ar	ˌdrīvø̸
çall̸'er	saı̸l'or	bĕḡ'ḡar	ĕd'it
wõrk'er	ere ā'tor	sẽrv'ant	as sĭst'

The suffix **-er** also indicates the comparative degree of adjectives, and **-est** the superlative. Let the pupil compare in the same way the words in the last column.

străngø̸	strān'ḡer	strān'ḡest	ḡrāvø̸
blă¢k	blă¢k'er	blă¢k'est	fạlsø̸
chē¢p	chē¢p'er	chē¢p'est	seârçø̸

Lesson 210.

TRADES AND OCCUPATIONS ENDING IN -ER.

păv'er	drŏv'er	plănt'er	ḡär'dø̸n er
bāk'er	c͞oōp'er	pāı̸nt'er	çăr'pen ter
põr'ter	bănk'er	prı̆nt'er	plås'ter er
ḡrō'çer	färm'er	bụtch'er	en ḡrāv'er
çärt'er	wĕạv'er	tē̤ạch'er	fär'ri er

Paver is also written păv'ier and păv'ior. A **porter** is a doorkeeper; also a carrier. **Porter** is also a malt liquor.

Lesson 211.

Adjectives ending in **y** generally form the comparatives and superlatives by changing the *y* into *i*, and adding *-er* and *-est*. Write the comparatives of the words in the last column.

hō′ly	hō′li er	hō′li est	mĕr′ry
ŭġ′ly	ŭġ′li er	ŭġ′li est	ċòmę′ly
sĭl′ly	sĭl′li er	sĭl′li est	rĕạ̈d′y

Words of more than two syllables are compared by prefixing **more** and **most**. Compare the words below, and fill blanks.

tĕr′ri blę̸ ĕx′çel lent wŏn′der fụl
bę̸aū′ti fụl ġlō′ri ø̸ūs tạlk′a tīvę̸

A circle is —— beautiful than a square. She was the —— excellent scholar of the two. He was the —— talkative boy in school.

Lesson 212.

maḷḷ, *a wooden hammer.*   aụ′ġer, *tool for boring.*
maụl, *to beat and bruise.*   aụ′ġur, *to foretell.*
haḷḷ, *a large room.*   ạl′tar, *place for sacrifice.*
haụl, *to pull or draw.*   ạl′ter, *to change; to vary.*
aụġḥt, *any thing.*   quạrts, *plural of* quart.
ȯụġḥt, *should; is fit.*   quạrtz, *a mineral; silex.*

aịl, aẉl. —— *shoemakers use an* ——.
baịl, baẉl.—*The earth is a* ——. *To* —— *is to cry aloud. A dancing-party is called a* ——.

Lesson 213.

The suffixes -er and -or denote the doer, and -ee the receiver.

pāy'er	pāy ēe'	lĕḡ a tôr'	lĕḡ a tēe'
dō'nor	do nēe'	as sĭgn ôr'	as sĭgn ēe'
lĕs'sor	lĕs sēe'	prŏm'is ôr	prŏm is ēe'
draw'er	draw ēe'	nŏm'i nôr	nŏm i nēe'
ḡrànt'or	ḡrànt ēe'	ḡuăr'an tôr	ḡuăr an tēe'

The **drawer** of an order or bill of exchange is the one who makes or draws it; the **drawee** the one on whom it is drawn. The **lessor** is the one who gives a lease; the **lessee** the one to whom it is given. The **legator** is one who bequeaths a legacy; the **legatee** receives it. **Conferree** is spelled with two **r's**.

Lesson 214.

NAMES OF VARIOUS KINDS OF TOOLS.

ăx	fīle	knīfe	hăm'mer	măl'let
hōe	rásp	lāthe	shŏv'el	trow'el
bit	spāde	brŭsh	chĭs'el	pĭck'ăx
saw	plāne	shēars	sĭck'le	erōw'-bär
ădz	flāil	slĕdge	ḡrāv'er	răm'mer
pĭck	wĕdge	squâre	măt'tock	eleav'er
rāke	ḡouḡe	ḡĭm'let	fôr'ceps	hătch'et

The seven principal hand-tools of civilized man are said to be the **ax, saw, plane, hammer, square, chisel,** and **file.**

Ye who long for work of nobler mold,
Oh, learn how common things may aid;
Whoever digs for diamonds or gold
Must needs use first—an iron spade.

P. S. B.—7.

Lesson 215.

The suffix **-en** means *to make;* as **harden,** *to make hard.*

härd'ẹn	shärp'ẹn	swēẹt'ẹn	whīt'ẹn
siẹk'ẹn	brīght'ẹn	blăẹk'ẹn	slăẹk'ẹn
dĕạd'ẹn	shôrt'ẹn	chēạp'ẹn	lōōs'ẹn

The suffix **-en** also means *made of;* as **wooden,** *made of* wood.

wŏŏd'ẹn	lĕạd'ẹn	ēạrth'ẹn	hĕmp'ẹn
wŏŏl'en	ăsh'ẹn	bīrch'ẹn	ōạt'ẹn
bēẹch'ẹn	ōạk'ẹn	sīlk'ẹn	whēạt'ẹn

We **deaden** the motion of a ship, and the speed **slackens**.
Loosen and **unloosen** mean the same; the latter is unnecessary.

Lesson 216.

âịr, *the atmosphere.*
ê'ẹr, *contraction of* ever.
êrẹ, *before; sooner than.*
hêịr, *one who inherits.*
bârẹ, *naked; empty.*
bẹâr, *animal; to carry.*
fâịr, *clear; handsome.*
fârẹ, *to travel; food.*
g̃lâịr, *white of an egg.*
g̃lârẹ, *dazzling light.*

hârẹ, *an animal.*
hâịr, *of the head.*
wẹâr, *to consume by use.*
wârẹ, *goods; mdse.*
stâịr, *a step of a series.*
stârẹ, *to look earnestly.*
târẹ, *an allowance.*
tẹâr, *to rend; lacerate.*
thêịr, *belonging to them.*
thêrẹ, *in that place.*

pârẹ, pẹâr, pâịr.—*He wanted to ——— the luscious Seckel ——— for the newly married ———.*

Lesson 217.

The suffix **-less** means *without*, as **hopeless**, *without* hope; **-ful** signifies *full of*, as **fearful**, *full of* fear; **-ly** means *like*, as **friendly**, like a friend; and **-ness**, *state* or *condition*, as **greenness**, *state* of being green. Define the words below as shown above.

trăck'lesṣ skĭll'fụl măn'ly sŏft'nesṣ
hōmḙ'lesṣ grāçḙ'fụl prĭnçḙ'ly swēḙt'nesṣ
housḙ'lesṣ spītḙ'fụl prīest'ly brīght'nesṣ

The suffix **-ly** is also a termination of adverbs signifying *manner*, and **-some** in certain adjectives indicates *a considerable degree*. The suffix **-y** denotes possession, as *mighty*, possessing might.

quĭck'ly glăd'somḙ nēḙd'y hōmḙ'ward
brīsk'ly wĭn'somḙ rŏck'y sēạ'ward
clĕạn'ly whōlḙ'somḙ hḙärt'y out'ward

Lesson 218.

Fill out the blanks below from the synonyms in this lesson.

pain   dĭs tresṣ'   ăn'guish   tôrt'ūrḙ
pärt   pōr'tion   frăe'tion   sĕe'tion
pāy   re ward'   wā'ges   stī'pend
gāin   mŏn'ḙў   rĭch'es   măm'mon
zēạl   är'dor   fēr'vor   fēḙl'ing
zĕst   rĕl'ish   flā'vor   sā'vor

We should be careful to —— our debts. She received a —— of merit. The workmen earned their ——. The minister labored for a settled ——.

Lesson 219.

The suffix **-ment** denotes condition, state, or act. It is a termination of nouns, formed often from verbs.

re tīre'ment är'ġu ment ae quire'ment
a bāse'ment con fīne'ment ar ränġe'ment
re frĕsh'ment com mĕnçe'ment ap point'ment

The suffix **-ance** means *state of being*, or *act of*.

de fī'ançe as sĭst'ançe for bęâr'ançe
al lī'ançe an noy'ançe re mŏn'strançe
con trīv'ançe at tĕnd'ançe ae quāịnt'ançe

Though Conversation, in its better part
May be esteemed a gift, and not an art;
Yet much depends, as in the tiller's toil,
On culture, and the sowing of the soil.

Lesson 220.

WORDS PERTAINING TO STREAMS AND BODIES OF WATER.

bär pŏnd shŏal straịt răp'ids
bāy pōol brŏok strẹạm dĕl'ūġe
rŭn lāke swạmp brànch eûr'rent
ġŭlf wāve sound rĭv'er chăn'nel
cōve rĭlỵ bănks ĭn'let eas cāde'
fōrd tīde shŏre bạỹ'ọu shăl'lōẉs

The **stream** was not an **inlet** from the **ocean**, nor a **bayou** from the lake, but a running **brook**. The **Banks** of Newfoundland are **shoals** or **shallows** in the **sea**, and are covered with water. The **current** in the **channel** is generally rapid. A *mere* is a **lake**.

Lesson 221.

The suffixes **-et, -let, -ling, -ule,** and **-ette** mean *little*.

iṣ'let	gŏṣ'ling	çĕl'lūl/	çĭḡ a rĕt//'
e/ḡlet	dŭ/k'ling	ḡlŏb'ūl/	stăt ū ĕt/''
çīr'elet	lôrd'ling	sphĕr'ūl/	nŏv el ĕt/''

The suffixes **-dom, -hood, -ship,** and **-age** mean *state of being*.

frē/'dŏm	boy'hōōd	lôrd'ship	bŏnd'ȧḡ/
king'dŏm	gīrl'hōōd	härd'ship	pē/r'aḡ/
ē/rl'dŏm	măn'hōōd	elērk'ship	coin'aḡ/

The suffix **-ish** means *like, of,* or *pertaining to*, and quality in a small degree; **-ess** indicates the feminine gender of some nouns.

thịēv'ish	Dān'ish	swē/t'ish	ḡŏd'dess
elown'ish	Rōm'ish	rĕd'dish	ĕm'pres$
fịēnd'ish	Seŏt'tish	ḡrāy''ish	ȧet'res$

Lesson 222.

wȧịt, *to stay; to rest.*
weị́ght, *heaviness; load.*
ḡāḡ/, *a pledge or pawn.*
ḡāụḡ/, *to measure.*
wāy', *course; direction.*
weị́gh, *to take the weight.*

plāịn, *without ornament.*
plānẹ, *level; flat; even.*
plāịt, *a fold; a braid.*
plātẹ, *flattened metal.*
nāvẹ, *body of a church.*
knāvẹ, *a rogue; villain.*

rȧịn, rẹịn, reị́gn.—The —— *fell in torrents.* He broke the —— *of his bridle.* Queen Victoria's —— *has extended over fifty years.*

Lesson 223.

The suffixes **-able** and **-ible** mean *able to be,* or *fit to be.*

eūr'a blé	ăd'mi ra blé	dī vĭṣ' i blé
loṣ'a blé	mĕm'o ra blé	re dū'çi blé
nām'a blé	tŏl'er a blé	dī ġĕst'i blé

The suffix **-ion** means *the act of,* or *state of being.*

eon něe'tion	eon vŭl'sion	ĕd ū eā'tion
in věn'tion	eon fū'ṣion	prŏs e eū'tion
in strūe'tion	dif fū'ṣion	ĕs ti mā'tion

Education is from Latin *e*, out, and *ducere*, to lead; hence to **educate** is to lead or draw out, and the process implies more the training of the mind than the communication of knowledge.

Lesson 224.

WORDS PERTAINING TO THE AIR.

eāÿm	whiff	brēęzę	tor nā'do
ġŭst	blăst	zĕph'yr	trădę'-wĭnd
ġālę	stôrm	çȳ'elōnę	whĭrl'wĭnd
wĭnd	squalł	tĕm'pest	hŭr'ri eānę
blōẃ	brĕạth	blĭz'zard	ăt'mos phĕrę

Fair laughs the morn, and soft the —— blows.

A **gale** is a wind between a stiff **breeze** and a **tempest**. A **zephyr** is the west wind, but is applied to any soft, mild, gentle breeze. A **gust** is a fierce **blast**; a **blizzard** a sudden, violent *snow-storm;* and a **cyclone** a powerful **whirlwind**.

Lesson 225.

The suffix **-ous** means *full of,* or *given to;* as **furious,** *full of fury*: **-ive** means *able to,* or *having power to*: **-ic** means *of,* or *pertaining to,* or *tending to;* as **tyrannic,** *pertaining to a tyrant.*

fū′ri ǿŭs	pro tĕet′ĭvǿ	des pŏt′ie
vĕn′om ǿŭs	suḡ ġĕst′ĭvǿ	dra măt′ie
poi′sǿn ǿŭs	op prĕss′ĭvǿ	he rō′ie

The suffixes of the words in the first and third columns mean *pertaining to,* and their meaning may be found by prefixing *pertaining to* to the words of the second and fourth columns; as **maniac,** *pertaining to* madness.

mā′ni ăe	măd′ness	lĭt′er a ry	lĕt′ters
mū′sie al	mū′sie	ĭn′fan tīlǿ	ĭn′fant
fĕm′i nĭnǿ	fē′mālǿ	pĭs′ea to ry	fĭsh′es
pŏp′ū lar	pēǿ′plǿ	hȳ me nē′an	măr′riǻgǿ

Lesson 226.

SYNONYMS.

fēat	ĕx′ploit	ăet	a chȳēvǿ′ment
fīght	băt′tlǿ	frāy	en ḡāḡǿ′ment
fǿūd	quạr′rel	broil	eon tĕn′tion
flăt	văp′id	stālǿ	in sĭp′id
foil	băf′flǿ	baḷk	dĭs ap point′
fōōd	dī′et	fârǿ	ăl′i ment
frăṉk	ō′pǿn	frēǿ	ŭn re sērvǿd′

A **feat** is a deed well done; an **exploit** is a heroic act; an **act** is simply a *deed;* and an **achievement** a great or heroic deed.

Lesson 227.

The terminations of the following words comprise nearly all the suffixes signifying *one who*, or *one skilled in*, and may be defined as in **artist**, *one skilled in art;* or **trustee**, *one to whom a trust is given.* Note also the pronunciation of **financier**.

ärt'ist	eăp'tĭvȩ	fā'vor ĭtȩ
trus tēȩ'	slŭḡ'ḡard	fĭn an çīer'
erĭt'ie	plaínt'iff	lăp'i da ry
laẃ'yer	eon sīḡn'or	hıs tō'ri an
stū'dent	çĭt'i zen	bĕn e fāe'tor
vā'ḡrant	ăd'vo eātȩ	bī ŏḡ'ra pher
tēȧm'ster	bŏt'a nĭst	chăr i ot ēȩr'

Lesson 228.

Fill the blanks below, and form new sentences.

ûrn, *a vessel; a vase.*
ēȧrn, *to gain by labor.*
vălȩ, *a valley; a dell.*
veıl, *cover for the face.*
eȧst, *to throw; to hurl.*
eȧstȩ, *a class of society.*
stīlȩ, *steps over a fence.*
stȳlȩ, *choice of words.*
sweȩ́t, *agreeable taste.*

suïtȩ, *a retinue; series.*
vānȩ, *a weather-cock.*
vaı́n, *empty; showy.*
veı̇n, *a blood-vessel.*
ī'dlȩ, *useless; lazy.*
ī'dol, *image of a god.*
ī'dyl, *a pastoral poem.*
kēẏ, *that which unlocks.*
quay (kē), *a wharf.*

rītȩ, ẃrītȩ, rīḡ)ĭt, ẃrīḡ)ĭt.—*The ship*——, *although unable to read or* ——, *performed the* —— *gracefully, and it was thought quite* ——.

SPELLER. 105

Lesson 229.

WORDS DERIVED FROM THE LATIN.

ălp	ḡaṉd	păet	dĕnsø̸	spīkø̸
dăb	ḡlŭt	stŏp	dīgh̸t	străp
eŭp	jĭlt	tăet	dĭrḡø̸	ăx'ĭs
pēø̸	lĕns̤	ûrḡø̸	frŏnd	dī'al
eōop	lĭnt	vōtø̸	blănk	o mĭt'
eûrt	mĭlȲ	erĭsp	prọvø̸	pī'eȧ
dīrø̸	mōlt	elăng̅	shĭrk	vē'to
dŭet	nōdø̸	erēø̸d	sŏlvø̸	strĭet
făet	nūdø̸	erātø̸	spĕnd	chēø̸s̤ø̸

A **frond** is a leafy branch. **Spike** is from *spica*, an ear of corn, and means a *sharp point*, a *large nail*, or an *ear of corn*. A **node** is literally a *knot*, a term used in astronomy and other sciences.

Lesson 230.

Require the pupil to ascertain from what root-words in Lesson 229 the following words have been derived.

ḡaṉd'y	nū'dĭ ty	o mĭs'sion
ăl'pĭnø̸	dĕn'sĭ ty	pro bā'tion
dăb'bler	ûr'ḡcn çy	eōop'cr aḡø̸
dŭe'tĭlø̸	nŏd'ū lar	ḡlŭt'tø̸n ø̸ŭs
spīkø̸'let	tăet'ū al	strĭn'ḡent ly
erĭsp'ness̸	erĕd'ĭ blø̸	spĕnd'thrĭft

According to Lesson 221, what does **spikelet** mean? From Lesson 217, what meaning would you attach to **crispness** and **stringently**? From Lesson 209, what does **dabbler** mean?

Lesson 231.

PREFIXES.

A **prefix** is a letter, syllable, or word set before a word, or combined or united with it at its beginning, to vary its signification. The prefix **in-** signifies *not*, and takes the form of **ig-, il-, im-,** and **ir-** before certain consonants, as given below.

in ăet'ĭvę	ĭg nō'blę	ĭm'po tent
ĭn cor rĕct'	il lē'ḡal	im prŏp'er
ĭn com plētę'	im môr'tal	ir rĕḡ'ū lar

The prefix **in-** also means *within*; and the prefixes **un-** and **non-** mean *not*. As a verbal prefix **un-** expresses a reversal of the action indicated by the simple word. In this sense it appears in the third column.

ĭn'bôrn	un fĭt'	un tĭę'	nŏn'aḡę
ĭn'brĕd	un rīpę'	un bär'	nŏn'sūịt
ĭn clōsę'	un truę'	un bōlt'	nŏn'sensę

Lesson 232.

WORDS PERTAINING TO LAW.

plēạ	clāịm	jū'ry	at tŏr'nęy
cōdę	cōụrt	cli'ent	chàn'çe ry
writ	caụsę	di'ḡest	sub pœ'nȧ
sūịt	jŭdḡę	vēr'dict	prŏs'e cūtę
dēęd	chärḡę	shĕr'iff	de fĕnd'ant

A **subpœna** is a writ commanding a person to attend in court under a penalty; the second syllable is pronounced pē. A **digest** is a body of laws; to di ḡest' is to assimilate food; arrange.

Lesson 233.

The prefixes **fore-, pre-, ante-,** and **before-,** are synonymous.

fōrḙ sēḙ' pre çēdḙ' ăn'te rōōm
fōrḙ tĕll' pre jŭdġḙ' ăn'te dātḙ
fōrḙ knōw' pre fĭġ'ūrḙ be fōrḙ'hănd
fōrḙ'mōst prē or dāin' be fōrḙ'tīmḙ

Post-, first column, is English, and refers to the *mail;* in the second column it is Latin, and means *after.* The word **after** carries its own meaning both as a prefix and as a suffix.

pōst'al pōst'-dātḙ åft'er mōst
pōst'aġḙ pōst'-ĕn try åft'er ward
pōst'märk pos tē'ri or hērḙ åft'er
pōst'-ŏf fĭçḙ pōst-môr'tem thêrḙ åft'er

Lesson 234.

wĕth'er, *a sheep.* | mĕd'al, *a special coin.*
wĕ*a*th'er, *state of the air.* | mĕd'dlḙ, *to interfere with.*
kẽrn'el, *part of a nut.* | ŏt'ter, *the water-weasel.*
eȯlḙ'nel, *an army officer.* | ŏt'tar, *oil of roses.*
măn'ner, *form; fashion.* | pĕd'al, *lever for the foot.*
măn'or, *a district; estate.* | pĕd'dlḙ, *to carry for sale.*
mĕt'al, *iron, lead, etc.* | sūe'eor, *help; aid; relief.*
mĕt'tlḙ, *spirit; ardor.* | sŭḙk'er, *a shoot; a fish.*

mīn'er, mī'nor.—*The digger of metals was a* ———, *but his son, being a* ———, *could not vote.*

Lesson 235.

The prefixes **one-** (Eng.), **uni-** (Lat. *unus*, one), and **mono-** (Gr. *monos*, one), have the same meaning.

one'ness (wun-)	ū'ni ty	mŏn'o ḡrăm
one'-hôrse	ū'ni fȳ	mŏn'o tōne
one'-ärmed	ū'ni sòn	mo nŏp'o ly
one'-sīd ed	ū'ni fôrm	mo nŏt'o nøŭs

The prefixes **two-** (Eng.), **twi-** (Anglo-Saxon), **bi-** (Lat. *bis*, twice), and **duo** (Lat.), have the same meaning.

two'fōld	bī'fôrm	dū'al
two'-pĕnçe	bī'vălve	dū'plex
twī'līḡ}ĭt	bī'çȳ ele	dū'pli eate
twĭn'-bôrn	bī ĕn'ni al	du plĭç'i tȳ

Lesson 236.

WORDS FROM THE GREEK.

bäl'm	eŏach	ăt'om	pō'sy	çē'dar
eōne	châ̟ir	çeḽ'o	eō'mà	bī'son
pŏmp	eŭpse	ĕp'ie	pō'et	dĕv'ĭl
tomb	păste	lā'ie	pĕt'al	ôr'ḡan
plāçe	lärch	ō'nyx	a bȳss'	ăt'las
trōpe	chīme	ī'ris	eā'lyx	nŏm'ad
trout	ăl'ōe	pō'em	ăn'ḡel	ăḡ'ate

Point out the *nine* words in the above lesson which refer to trees, plants, and flowers; the *four* which refer to rhetoric and literature; and the *two* that are the names of stones.

Lesson 237.

The prefixes **tre-, tri-** (Lat.), and **three-**, are synonymous.

thrēe'-plȳ   trē'foil   trī'an ḡle
thrēe'fōld   trĕb'ly   trī'eol or
thrēe'-sīd ed   trĭn'i ty   trī ĕn'ni al

The prefixes **quad-, quar-** (Lat.), and **four-**, are synonymous.

fōur'fōld   quạr'to   quạd'rụ ped
fōur'seōre   quạr'ter   quạd'rụ ple
fōur'fōot ed   quạd'rate   quạd rĕn'ni al

Lesson 238.

AMERICANISMS.

OF INDIAN ORIGIN.

māize   ea noe'   wĭḡ'wạm   to băe'eo
mōōse   ḡuä'no   quī'nīne   o pŏs'sum
skŭnk   rae eōōn'   mŏe'ea sin   hŏm'i ny

OF SPANISH ORIGIN.

rănch   lăs'so   mŭs'tang   lăr'i at
plä'zä   brŏn'eo   ḡar rōte'   bo năn'zȧ
pla çêr'   erē'ōle   a dō'be   pụ eb'lo

OF FRENCH ORIGIN.

būtte   ḡō'pher   lĕv'ee   quạd rōōn'
eăçhe   pōrt'aḡe   ere văsse'   eăl'ū mĕt
çhụte   prāi'rie   la erŏsse'   bär'be eūe

Lesson 239.

The prefix **con-** means *with* or *together;* before certain letters it changes to **com-, col-, co-, cog-,** and **cor-,** as below.

con join′	com mĭx′	cō hēre̸′	cor rĕet′
con fīrm′	com pōṣe̸′	cō ērçe̸′	cor rōde̸′
con fôrm′	com mànd′	cŏḡ′nāte̸	cŏr rc lāte̸′
con dĕnse̸′	com pound′	cŏḡ′nīze̸	cŏr re spŏnd′

The prefix **ad-** signifies *to,* and is changed to **af-, al-, an-, ap-, as-,** and **at-,** before certain consonants, as in the following.

ad mĭx′	af fīrm′	an nĕx′	as sāi̸l′
ad join′	af frīgḥt′	an nūl′	as sūre̸′
ad jŭst′	al lāy̸′	ap pĕnd′	at tĕst′
ăd′verb	al lŏt′	ap pĕa̸r′	at tāi̸n′

Lesson 240.

WORDS FROM THE DUTCH LANGUAGE.

tŏp	snăp	clămp	hoist	a lōōf′
bōōr	swạb	ḡrowl	ḡrōōve̸	brụ′in
dĕlf	yạw̸l	ḡrŭff̸	splĭçe̸	wăḡ′on
ḡŭlf	dŏc̸k	mŭmps	strīpe̸	dăp′per
kĭn̠k	rōve̸	slōōp	swĭt̸ch	rŭf′fle̸
mōpe̸	ō′ḡle̸	stōve̸	stránd	frŏl′ic
rănt	blŭff̸	foist	c lōpe̸′	brăn′dy

Which words in the above show the Dutch to have been a sea-faring people? Which words indicate action? Which one means a peasant? Which sound occurs seven times?

Lesson 241.

The prefixes **half-** (Eng.), **semi-** (Lat.), **hemi-** (Gr.), and **demi-** (Fr.), have the same meaning. The following are illustrations.

hä̆lf'-mōon	sĕm'ĭ quā ver	hĕm'i sphēr¢
hä̆lf'-prīç¢	sĕm'ĭ çīr €l¢	dĕm'i-ḡŏd
hä̆lf'-pĕn ny	sĕm ĭ-ăn'nu al	dĕm'i-bäth

Trans- means *across*, or *beyond;* **circum-**, *around;* and **super-**, *above*, or *over*. All these prefixes are from the Latin.

trans fôrm'	çīr'€um stanç¢	sū'per fīn¢
trans plănt'	çīr €um pō'lar	su pēr'flu ∅ŭs
trans ălp'ĭn¢	çir €ŭm'fer enç¢	su pēr'la tĭv¢

Which word means to plant in a new place? Which means the boundary of a circle? Which means in the highest degree?

Lesson 242.

MEASURES OF VARIOUS KINDS.

tón	spăn	ḫour	ḡrā̇n	sĕe'ond
ġĭll̀	pāç¢	wĕ¢k	ounç¢	ḡăl'lon
pīnt	lĭnk	rē∂m	quạrt	buṣh'el
ĭnch	rōōd	chā̇n	mónth·	de ḡrēe'
yärd	yē∂r	seōr¢	dóz'¢n	fäth'om
mīl¢	€ôrd	ḡrōss̀	lē∂ḡu¢	fûr'long̀
nā̇l	pĕ¢k	pērch	€ū'bit	seru̇'pl¢

Do you covet learning's prize?
Climb her heights and take it.
In ourselves our fortune lies;
Life is what we make it.

Lesson 243.

Pro- means *for*, or *forth;* **re-,** *back*, or *again;* **per-,** *through;* and **e-,** or **ex-,** *out of.* All these prefixes are Latin.

pro pĕl′	re ăct′	per vādĕ′	e jĕct′
pro lŏng′	re join′	per tûrb′	ē′g̃ress
prō′noun	re bu̇ïld′	per fôrm′	ex̱ hālĕ′

Dis- (Lat.) means *not*, or *apart;* **a-,** or **ab-,** (Lat.) *from, away;* **en-,** (Fr. **en**; Lat. **in**) *to make*, or *put in;* before *p* and *b* it becomes **em-**.

dis̱ ärm′	a void′	en ăct′	em bärk′
dis bănd′	a vẽrt′	en rĭch′	em bäl′m′
dis join′	ab sŏlvĕ′	en slāvĕ′	em pow′er

Lesson 244.

WORDS SOMETIMES MISUNDERSTOOD OR MISUSED.

bōu̱rn, *a bound, a limit,—not a country.*
ō′ral, *spoken,* not *written.*
vẽr′bal, *expressed in words; literal.*
elĕv′er, *possessing skill.*
al lūdĕ′, *to hint at.*
bûrst, not '*bursted.*'
eou̇p′lĕ, *two things joined together; a pair.*
trans pīrĕ′, *to become public; to ooze out.*

moi′e ty, *the half,—not a small part.* [or *ill.*
de mēan′, *to behave, well*
tru̱′eu lent, *fierce, wild, savage,—*not *truckling.*
prĕd′i eātĕ, *to affirm,— not to base upon.*
al tẽr′na tĭvĕ, *a choice between two things only.*
illY, '*illy*' *is improper.*
sus pĕct′ed, '*suspicioned*' *is improper.*

SPELLER.   113

Lesson 245.

Anti-, contra-, and **counter-** mean *against, in opposition to.*

ăn'tĭ dōtĕ̸   eŏn tra dĭet'   eoun ter ăet'
an tĭp'a thy   eŏn'tra bănd   eoun'ter fĕ̸ĭt
an tĭth'e sĭs eŏn tra vēnĕ̸'   eoun ter mànd'

Inter- means *between, among;* **intro-,** *in, within;* and **multi-,** *many.*

ĭn ter fēr$\not{e}$'   ĭn tro dūç$\not{e}$'   mŭl'tĭ pl$\not{e}$
ĭn ter jĕet'   ĭn tro vērt'   mŭl'tĭ fôrm
ĭn ter çēd$\not{e}$'   ĭn tro spĕet'   mŭl'tĭ foil

Lesson 246.

From the suffixes explained in this lesson, give the meaning of the words in Lesson 245: as **antidote,** *anti,* against, *dotos,* given; hence, a remedy given against poison, etc. The first three words are Greek; the others Latin.

dō'tŏs, *given.*   fe rī're, *to strike.*
pa thĕ̸ĭn', *to suffer.*   jăç'e re, *to cast.*
thē'sĭs, *a setting.*   çĕd'e re, *to go.*
dĭç'e re, *to speak.*   dū'çe re, *to lead.*
băn'dum, *a ban.*   vēr'te re, *to turn.*
ve nī're, *to come.*   spĕç'e re, *to look.*
ăe'tum, *to act.*   plĭ eā're, *to fold.*
făç'e re, *to make.*   fôr'mà, *shape.*
man dā're, *to command.*   fō'lĭ um, *a leaf.*

The, alone or emphasized, is pronounced thē; in reading it is changed to thĭ or thŭ. **A,** in reading, is changed to ă or ŭ.

Lesson 247.

EXERCISES IN WORD-CONSTRUCTION.

Change the following adjectives to adverbs, according to Lesson 217: as, **candid, candidly; honest, honestly;** etc.

căn'did	po līt*ẹ*'	stĕạ́d'y	ob sẹ̄ēnẹ̄'
hŏn'est	pre çīsẹ'	pŏmp'ǿŭs	splĕn'did

Change these adjectives to nouns, according to Lesson 217.

tī'dy	dĭz'zy	hăp'py	wāk*ẹ*'fu̇l
lŏft'y	hĕạ́v'y	ĕmp'ty	chē*ẹ*r'fu̇l

Change the following verbs to nouns, according to Lesson 219.

a mūs*ẹ*'	pŭn'ish	ar răṅġ*ẹ*'	im pē*ạ́*ch'
in dūç*ẹ*'	sĕt'tl*ẹ*	con tĕnt'	nǿŭr'ish

Change the following nouns to adjectives, according to Lesson 225; as **riot, riotous,** etc.

rī'ot	pĕr'il	hăz'ard	slăn'der
hū'mor	rīḡ'or	mär'vel	ḡlŭt'tǿn

Lesson 248.

Find a synonym in Lesson 247 for each word in this lesson: as, **wit, humor; neat, tidy; gormand, glutton;** etc.

wĭt	dĭ vẽrt'	wŏn'der	nûrt'ūr*ẹ*
nēặt	līv*ẹ*'ly	sin çēr*ẹ*'	chas tīs*ẹ*'
fĭx*ẹ*d	ae eūs*ẹ*'	re fīn*ẹ*d'	ḡôr'mand
shōẉ'y	ŭp'rō*ạ*r	stāt*ẹ*'ly	stĭff'nes*s*
hŏl'lōẉ	dăn'ger	blĕs*s*'ed	weiḡḥt'y

Lesson 249.

Sub- (Lat.) means *under* or *below;* it is changed to **suc-, suf-, sus-, sup-,** and **sur-,** for smoothness of pronunciation. **Sur-** is also a contraction of **super-** (Lat.), *upon, above, beyond.*

sub dūe'	sue eŭmb'	sup pōrt'	sur vīve'
sub join'	sue çēed'	sup piănt'	sûr'façe
sub vẽrt'	suf fĭx'	sus tāin'	sur pàss'
sub mẽrġe'	suf fūse'	sus pĕnd'	sur mount'

De- means *from* or *down;* **mis-,** *wrong;* and **out-** and **up-** carry their own meaning. The first two are Latin; the last two English.

de fĕnd'	mis dāte'	out rănk'	up bēâr'
de dūet'	mis tāke'	out sāil'	up hōld'
de fāme'	mis lĕad'	out ġrōw'	up lĭft'
de frayd'	mis spĕll'	out shīne'	up hĕave'

Lesson 250.

THE SEVEN SAGES OF GREECE, AND THEIR MAXIMS.

1. Bī'as—"*Most men are bad*"; 2. Chī'lo—"*Consider the end*"; 3. Clē o bū'lus—"*Avoid extremes*"; 4. Pē ri ăn'der—"*Nothing is impossible to industry*"; 5. Pĭt'ta eus—"*Know thy opportunity*"; 6. Sō'lon —"*Know thyself*"; 7. Thā'lēs—"*Suretyship is the forerunner of ruin.*"

Shakespeare, who displayed a greater variety of expression than probably any writer in any language, produced all his plays with about 15,000 words. Milton's works are built up with 8,000; and the Old Testament says all that it has to say with 5,642 words. Ninety-three per cent of Bunyan's words are Saxon.

Lesson 251.

EXERCISE IN SUFFIXES.

Make adjectives out of the following words by suffixing **-able** or **-ible**, as the word may demand. See Lesson 223.

al low'	de dūçe'	com mĕnd'	dif fūse'
hŏn'or	re vērse'	re spĕet'	de fĕnse'

Make nouns out of these verbs, according to Lesson 223.

die'tāte	pro tĕet'	se lĕet'	nar rāte'
vī'brāte	dis tôrt'	con fĕss'	sub trăet'

Make nouns out of these verbs, according to Lesson 219.

an noy'	re sĭst'	in sụre'	con trīve'
at tĕnd'	sub sĭst'	dis tûrb'	de lĭv'er

Lesson 252.

CONTRACTIONS USED IN CONVERSATION AND POETRY.

I'm = *I am.*	e'en = *even.*	who'd = *who would.*
I'll = *I will.*	o'er = *over.*	won't = *will not.*
I've = *I have.*	e'er = *ever.*	we've = *we have.*
cän't = *can not.*	ne'er = *never.*	you're = *you are.*
dŏn't = *do not.*	'tis = *it is.*	shä'n't = *shall not.*
'twas = *it was.*	it's = *it is.*	you've = *you have.*
we'll = *we will.*	he's = *he is.*	does n't = *does not.*
'twill = *it will.*	let's = *let us.*	are n't = *are not.*
what's = *what is.*	is n't = *is not.*	there's = *there is.*

Lesson 253.

COMPOUND WORDS USED BY SHAKESPEARE.

out-her'od un pāïd'-fôr grĭm'-vĭṣ aġėd
ġrēėn'-ėȳėd snăp'per-ŭp thĭċk'-com ing
twiċė'-tōld stĭlľ'-vĕxėd stĭċk'ing-plāċė
pālė'-fāċėd wŏrk'ing-dāy̆ sĕlf-slạu̇ġh'ter
cloud'-eăpt hâi̇̆r'-brĕặdth trŭmp'et-tóngu̇ėd

Lesson 254.

FAMILIAR QUOTATIONS FROM SHAKESPEARE.

The words of Lesson 253 are given below, with the name of the play in which they are found. Let the teacher require the correct spelling and the meaning of the words used.

It *out-herods* Herod.—*Hamlet.* The *green-eyed* monster.—*Othello.* A *twice-told* tale.—*King John.* The *pale-faced* moon.—*King Henry IV.* The *cloud-capt* towers.—*The Tempest.* Rustling in *unpaid-for* silk.—*Cymbeline.* A *snapper-up* of unconsidered trifles.—*The Winter's Tale.* The *still-vexed* Bermoothes.—*The Tempest.* This *working-day* world.—*As You Like It.* *Hair-breadth* 'scapes.—*Othello.* *Grim-visaged* war.—*Richard III.* Troubled with *thick-coming* fancies.—*Macbeth.* Screw your courage to the *sticking-place.*—*Macbeth.* His canon 'gainst *self-slaughter.*—*Hamlet.* Like angels, *trumpet-tongued.*—*Macbeth.*

Lesson 255.

EXERCISE IN PREFIXES.

Prefix **in-** in its proper form before the following words, and then define them according to Lesson 231; as, **valid**, *invalid*.

văl'id	mŏr'al	cŏn'stant	pā'tient
hū'man	mē'di atę́	dis tīṉet'	pär'tial
cau̇'tiǫus	mū'ta blę́	rĕv'er ent	prŏp'er
dis crēęt'	mŏd'er atę́	rĕṣ'o lūtę́	prŏb'ablę́

Place the prefix before these meaning *before* (Lesson 233).

gō'ing	pos sĕsṣ'	tō'kę́n	ma tūrę́'
rŭn'ner	dĕs'tinę́	or dāịn'	de tēr'mĭnę́
shăd'ōw̨	mĕd'i tātę́	tĕll'er	ĕm'i nent
mĕn'tion	rĕq'ui ṣītę́	warn'ing	dōm'i nātę́

Lesson 256.

Place the prefix to these meaning *with* or *together* (Lesson 239).

strāịn	miṉ'glę́	ef fi'cient	re lātę́'
trīb'ūtę́	mĭs'sion	ŏp'er ātę́	rŭp'tion
sē'quençę́	păs'sion	e tēr'nal	re spŏnd'ent

Place before these the prefix that means *wrong* (Lesson 249).

eăr'ry	in fôrm'	eon çēịvę́'	trŭst'fu̇l
măn'aġę́	em ploy'	pro nounçę́'	stātę́'ment
be hāvę́'	eăr'riaġę́	spĕll'ing	ad vĕnt'ūrę́

From the Spectator: My lords, with humble submission that that I say is this, that that that that gentleman has advanced is not that that he should have proved to your lordships.

SPELLER. 119

REVIEW OF SUFFIXES.

Give the signification of the various Suffixes.

Lesson 257.

height'en	noise'less	bail ee'
straight'en	friend'less	ab sen tee'
a wāk'en	ceas'less	môrt ga gee'
be hōld'en	breath'less	eon sign ee'
eav'il er	a bet'tor	reg'is trar
chăl'len ger	as sess'or	as sist'ant
de mûr'rer	cel'e bra tor	af firm'ant
de sign'er	eal'eu la tor	ad hēr'ent
ăn'a lyz er	em băs'sa dor	eom plain'ant
eon vey'an cer	eon trib'ū tor	eom man dänt'

Lesson 258.

dū'ti ful	a līgn'ment	ärm'let
făn'çi ful	a gree'ment	pī pett'e
pit'i ful	al low'ançe	ro sett'e
maid'en ly	ae eôrd'ançe	par quett'e
wom'an ly	per fôrm'ançe	found'ling
sōl'dier ly	flow'er et	fŏs'ter ling
awk'ward ness	băs'çi net	ŭn'der ling
pret'ti ness	cel la rĕt'	mŏl'e eūle
right'eous ness	riv'ū let	rĕt'i eūle
gŏv'ern ment	eov'er let	ăn i măl'eūle

REVIEW OF SUFFIXES. (Continued.)

Give the signification of the various Suffixes.

Lesson 259.

sour'ish	ḩêir'ess	pr̯iēst'hŏŏd
ķnāv'ish	prĭn'çess	mā̯i̇d'ḝn hŏŏd
whīt'ish	ġī'ant ess	wĭd'ō w̑ hŏŏd
quäl̯m'ish	ḡŏv'ern ess	neig̑ḩ'bor hŏŏd
squē a̯m'ish	en chȧnt'ress	băch'e lor hŏŏd
sẽrf'dŏm	vĭç'i naġḝ	çĕn'sor shĭp
prĭnçḝ'dŏm	vẽr'bi aġḝ	pärt'ner shĭp
mär'tyr dŏm	lĭn'e aġḝ	seḩŏl'ar shĭp
hḙx̯'thḝn dŏm	fō'li aġḝ	die tā'tor shĭp
eḩ̯rĭs'tḝn dŏm	au̯eḩ'or aġḝ	ap prĕn'tĭçḝ shĭp

Lesson 260.

ăf'fa blḝ	a vẽr'sion	ɇon ɇlū'sĭvḝ
ɇā'pa blḝ	ɇon dĭ'tion	trăn'si tīvḝ
ɇūl'pa blḝ	ex păn'sion	de çī'sĭvḝ
ā'mi a blḝ	hĕs̱ i tā'tion	lū'era tīvḝ
pēr'me a blḝ	ĭn tu ĭ'tion	ɇon dū'çĭve
sĕn'si blḝ	of fĭ'cĭḝus	fa nă t'ie
făl'li blḝ	am bĭ'tiḝus	la ɇŏn'ie
tăn'ġi blḝ	plĕn'te ḝus	pa thĕt'ie
fḙx̯'si blḝ	stū'di ḝus	dī dăe'tie
re spŏn'si blḝ	tȳr'an nḝus	ter̄rĭf'ic

SPELLER.

REVIEW OF PREFIXES.

Indicate the signification of the various Prefixes.

Lesson 261.

in ea'pa blȩ	fōrȩ elōṣ'ūrȩ	mo nŏp'o līzȩ
in eo hēr'ençȩ	fōrȩ ḳnŏẘl'edġȩ	mŏn o līth'ie
ĭg̈'no mĭn y	prĕj ū dĭ'cial	trī ă<u>n</u>'g̈u lar
ĭg̈ no rā'mus	pre rŏg̈'a tĭvȩ	trĭ sẙl'la blȩ
il lĭb'er al	ăn te çĕd'ent	trī ŭm'vi ratȩ
il lŏġ'ie al	ăn te nŭp'tial	trĭp li ea'tion
ĭm per fĕe'tion	pŏst'hu mø̆ŭs	qua̤r'tern
im prŏv'i dent	pōst pōnȩ'ment	qua̤r tĕtt̨ȩ'
ir ră'tion al	ū ni vērs'al	qua̤d ru̧'ma nø̆ŭs
ir rĕp'a ra blȩ	ū ni fôrm'i ty	qua̤d ră<u>n</u>'g̈u lar

Lesson 262.

eŏn çen trā'tion	eôr po rā'tion	ap pēa̲r'ançȩ
eon fĕd'er atȩ	eor rĕl'a tĭvȩ	ap prŏx'i mātȩ
eom mĕn'su rātȩ	ăd mo nī'tion	as sĕm'blag̈ȩ
eom mĭs'sion er	ăd ap tā'tion	as sō'ci atȩ
eol lĕet'ĭvȩ ly	af fĭḷ'i ātȩ	at tăch'ment
eol lăt'er al	af flĭe'tion	at trăe'tion
eo hēr'en çy	ăl li g̈ā'tion	dĕm'i-tīnt
eō ex̱ īst'ençȩ	al lŏt'ment	sĕm ĭ-lū'nar
eŏġ i tā'tion	an nī'hi lātȩ	sĕm ĭ-vō'eal
eŏg̈'ni za blȩ́	an nŭn'ci ātȩ́	sĕm ĭ çīr'eu lar

REVIEW OF PREFIXES. (*Continued.*)

Indicate the signification of the various Prefixes.

Lesson 263.

trăns'fer ençe̸	pro ḡrĕs'sion	dĭs ar rānḡe̸'ment
tra mŏn'tane̸	prŏp o ṣĭ'tion	dis eø̸ûr'te sy
trans vẽrse̸'ly	rĕe re ā'tion	āl ien ā'tion
çĩr eum serībe̸'	re eū'per āte̸	a nŏm'a lø̸ūs
çĩr eum vĕn'tion	pẽr me ā'tion	ăb di eā'tion
sū per in tĕnd'ent	pẽr fo rā'tion	ăb er rā'tion
sū per çĭl'i ø̸ūs	e măn'çi pāte̸	en vĕl'op ment
sur mount'a ble̸	e lĭm'i nāte̸	en eămp'ment
sur pàṣṣ'a ble̸	ĕx eul pā'tion	in dīçt'a ble̸
prŏe la mā'tion	ex pā'tri āte̸	ĭn flu ĕn'tial

Lesson 264.

em băr'raṣṣ ing	ĭn tro dŭe'tion	sus çĕp'ti ble̸
em bĕl'lish ment	ĭn tro spĕe'tion	sŭs'te nançe̸
an tĭp'o dal	mŭl ti tū'di nø̸ūs	sŭp plē mĕnt'al
ăn tĭ slāv'er y	mŭl ti fā'ri ø̸ūs	sŭp po ṣĭ'tion
eŏn tra dĭe'tion	sub ôr'di nate̸	sŭr ro ḡā'tion
eŏn'tra ri ly	sŭb ju ḡā'tion	sŭr rep ti'tiø̸ūs
eoun'ter poiṣe̸	sue çĕs'sion	de mŏr'al īze̸
eoun'ter sīgn	sue çĭṉet'ly	dē mar kā'tion
ĭn ter çĕs'sion	suf fĭ'cient ly	mĭs be hāv'ior
in tẽr'po lāte̸	sŭf fo eā'tion	mis ḡṇīd'ançe̸

Lesson 265.

COMPOUND WORDS FROM THE POETS.

Gŏd'-gĭv ĕn lī'on-hẽärt ma'nў-hĕad ed
mēĕk'-ĕyĕd lŏng'-drawn ma'nў-eòl'orĕd
stär'-ĕyĕd moōn'-strŭċk spīċĕ-ĭsl'andṣ
swạn'-līkĕ ĕạ'glĕ-ĕўĕ mȧs'ter-păs sion
wĕll'-brĕd grēĕn'-rōbĕd erĭm'sŏn-tĭppĕd

Lesson 266.

FAMILIAR QUOTATIONS.

The quotations below embody the words of Lesson 265. Used as a language exercise, the meaning of the words in italics should be required, together with brief accounts of the authors quoted; as *Burns*, a Scottish poet, born 1759, died 1796.

Wee, modest, *crimson-tipped* flower.—*Burns.* Profaned his *God-given* strength.—*Scott.* *Meek-eyed* Morn appears.—*Thomson.* O *star-eyed* Science. —*Campbell.* *Swan-like*, let me sing and die.—*Byron.* With a *well-bred* whisper close the scene.—*Cowper.* Lord of the *lion-heart* and *eagle-eye.*—*Smollett.* The *long-drawn* aisle and fretted vault.—*Gray.* *Moon-struck* madness.—*Milton.* One *master-passion* in the breast.—*Pope.* Those *green-robed* senators of mighty woods.—*Keats.* The *spice-islands* of youth and hope.—*Coleridge.* The *many-headed* monster of the pit.—*Massinger.* Life, like a dome of *many-colored* glass. —*Shelley.*

Lesson 267.

NAMES OF MEN.

Ā'bram	Âạr'on	Hăr'old	Ā'sȧ
A dŏlph'	Ăd'am	Hō'mer	Băṣ'il
Ġęôrġę	Ăl'bert	Hū'g̅o	Ƈā'leb
Hūġḥ	Ăn'drew	Ī'ṣaḍe	Çē'phas
Je rōmę'	Ƈlăr'ençę	Jăs'per	Çȳ'rus
Jōb	Dā'vid	Jō'ṣeph	Ęū'ġenę
Lūkę	Ĕd'ward	Lew'is	Fē'lix
Märk	Ĕd'win	Nō'ȧḥ	Jā'bez
Pạụl	Ĕz'rȧ	Păt'rĭçk	Lĕǿn'ard
Sạụl	Frȧn'çis	Pē'ter	Mō'ṣĕṣ
Rălph	G̅il'bert	Thŏm'as	Rō'land

Lesson 268.

INDIANA NAMES.

Bar thŏl'o mew	Căr'rolḷ	De ƈā'tur
Dā'vĭęsṣ	De Kălb'	Dējr'born
Dū bois'	Floyd	Fa yĕtṭę'
Hŭnt'ing tȯn	Hĕn'drĭçks	Jĕn'ningṣ
Jŏḥn'sȯn	Kŏs çi ŭs'ko-	La Pōrtę'
La G̅rānġę'	Lạw'rençę	Mī äm'i
Mā'ri on	Mär'shalḷ	Pŭt'nam
Pū lăs'ki	Stęū'ben	Swĭt'zer land
Sŭl'li van	Stärkę	Tĭp pe ƈa nǫę'
Ūn'ion	Văn'der bûrgḥ	Ver mĭl'lion
Wāy'nę	Wạr'rĭçk	Whītę'ly

Lesson 269.

NAMES OF WOMEN.

Ănńĕ	Ā'dȧ	Ĕs'tħer	Jō ăn'
Blȧnçhĕ	An nĕtŧĕ'	Ĕu'nĭçĕ	Jū'dĭth
Ēvĕ	Bō'nȧ	Ē'vȧ	Loŭ ïşĕ'
Grāçĕ	Bĕr'thȧ	Făn'ny	Lō'ĭs
Jān̄ĕ	Člăr'ĭçĕ	Flō'rȧ	Mā'bel
Jĕản	Čŏn'stançĕ	Frȧn'çes̄	Mär'thȧ
Kātĕ	Dō'rȧ	Gĕr'trudĕ	Mȳ'rȧ
Mańd	Ĕd'nȧ	Hăn'nȧħ	Năn'çy
Māy	Ĕm'mȧ	Hŭl'dȧħ	Rā'chel
Pĕărl	Fāĭth	Ī'dȧ	Rħō'dȧ
Ruth	Hĕs'ter	Ī'nez	Sū'şan

Lesson 270.

An gō'la	Ań'burn	Bōw'ling Grēĕn'
Côr'y dŏn	Dĕl'phi	Gō'shen
Ir ŏ quŏis'	Kăṉ'ka kēĕ	Kŏ'kŏ mŏ
Law'rençĕ burgħ	Lĕb'a nŏn	Max in kŭc'kēĕ
Mań mēĕ'	Mŏn ti çĕl'lŏ	Mŭn'çĭĕ
Mt. Vĕr'nŏn	Pa ō'li	Pe ru'
Plȳm'ŏŭth	Rŏch'es ter	Rĕns'se lăĕr
Shŏals̄	Spĕn'çer	Săl a mȧ'nĭĕ
Tĕr're Haute'(ōt)	Vĭn çĕnŋĭĕ's̄'	Väl pä rāī'sŏ
Ve vāy'	Ver sāĭlłĕs̄'	Wĭn'ches ter
Wĭn'a mae	Wȧ'bash	Wy an dŏtŧĕ'

Lesson 271.

The Thirteen Original States of the Union, with their Abbreviations, Capitals, and Dates of Settlement.

1607	Vĭr ġĭn'ĭ à	*Va.*	Rĭch'mònd
1613	New Yôrk'	*N. Y.*	Al'ba ny
1620	Măs sa chū'setts	*Mass.*	Bŏs'tòn
1623	New Hămp'shĭre	*N. H.*	Cŏn̠'eòrd
1633	Con nĕet'ĭ eut	*Conn.*	Härt'fôrd
1634	Mā'ry land	*Md.*	An năp'o lis
1636	Rhōde Isl'and	*R. I.*	{ Prŏv'i dençe New'pōrt
1638	Dĕl'a wâre	*Del.*	Dō'ver
1650	North Căr o lī'nà	*N. C.*	Ra̤'lĕĭġh
1664	New Jĕr'sey	*N. J.*	Trĕn'tòn
1670	South Căr o lī'nà	*S. C.*	Co lŭm'bĭ à
1682	Pĕnn sȳl vā'nĭ à	*Pa.*	Hăr'ris bûrg
1733	Gĕôr'ġĭ à	*Ga.*	At lăn'tà

Lesson 272.

Names of States, their Abbreviations, Capitals, and Dates of Admission into the Union.

1791	Ver mŏnt'	*Vt.*	Mont pē'lĭ er
1792	Ken tŭck'y	*Ky.*	Frănk'fort
1796	Tĕn nes sēe'	*Tenn.*	Năsh'vĭlle
1803	O hī'o	*O.*	Co lŭm'bus
1812	Lou ĭ sĭ à'nà	*La.*	Băt'òn Rŏuge (zh)
1816	In dĭ ăn'à	*Ind.*	In dĭ an ăp'o lis

Lesson 273.

1817	Mĭs sis sĭp'pĭ	Miss.		Jăçk'sŏn
1818	Ĭl'lĭ noĭs̨	Ill.		Sprĭng'fīēld
1819	Ăl a bà'mà	Ala.		Mont ḡŏm'er y̆
1820	Mā̤i̯'nę̆	Me.		A̤ŗ́ ḡŭs'tà
1821	Mĭs sǿu̯'rĭ	Mo.		Jĕff'er sŏn Çĭt'y̆
1836	Är'kan sa̤ş́	Ark.		Lĭt'tlę̆ Rŏçk
1837	Mĭçh'ĭ ḡan	Mich.		Lăn'sĭng
1845	Flŏr'ĭ dà	Fla.		Tăl la hăs'sę̆
1845	Tĕx'as	Tex.		A̤ŗ́s'tĭn
1846	Ī'o wà	Ia.		Deş́ Moĭnę̆ş́'
1848	Wĭs eŏn'sĭn	Wis.		Măd'ĭ sŏn
1850	Çăl ĭ fôr'nĭ à	Cal.		Săe ra mĕn'to
1858	Mĭn ne sō'tà	Minn.		Sā̤i̯nt Pa̤ŗ́l'

Lesson 274.

1859	Ŏr'e ḡȯn	Or.		Sā'lem
1861	Kăn'sas	Kan.		To pē'kà
1863	Wĕst Vĭr ḡĭn'ĭ à	W. Va.		Chärlę̆ş'tŏn
1864	Ne vä'dà	Nev.		Çär'sŏn Çĭt'y̆
1867	Ne brăs'kà	Neb.		Lĭṉ'eȯi̯n
1876	Çŏl̤ o rä'do	Col.		Dĕn'ver
1889	Nôrt̤h Da kō'tà	N. Dak.		Bĭş'märçk
1889	South Da kō'tà	S. Dak.		Pi ẹrŗ'ę̆'
1889	Mon tä'nà	Mon.		Hĕl'e nà
1889	Wa̤sh'ĭng tȯn	Wash.		O ly̆m'pĭ à
1890	Ī'da hō	Id.		Boĭ'sẹ Çĭt'y̆
1890	Wy̆ ō'mĭng	Wy.		Chey̆ ĕnŗ́ę̆'

Lesson 275.

Names of Territories with their Abbreviations, Capitals, and Dates of Organization.

1850	New Mĕx'i co	N. M.	Săn'tä Fẹ'
1850	Ū'taḫ	U. T.	Salt Lākẹ Çĭt'ȳ
1863	Ăr i zō'nȧ	Ar. T.	Phọ̄ē'nix
1867	Ā lăs'kȧ	Al. T.	Sĭt'kȧ
	Ĭnd'ian	Ind. T.	Tä}ḫ'le quȧḫ
1890	Ŏk la hō'mȧ	Okla. T.	Gŭth'rịe

Lesson 276.

NAMES OF THE PRESIDENTS.

Gẹôrgẹ Wạsh'ing tŏn
Jŏḫn Ăd'amṣ
Tḫŏm'as Jĕff'er sŏn
Jāmẹṣ Măd'i sŏn
Jāmẹṣ Mŏn rōẹ'
Jŏḫn Quĭn'çy Ăd'amṣ
Ăn'drew Jăẹk'sŏn
Mär'tin Văn Bū'ren
Wilḽ'iam Ḫ. Ḫăr'ri sŏn
Jŏḫn Tȳ'ler
Jāmẹṣ Knŏx Pŏḽk

Zăẹḫ'ȧ ḫ Tȳ'lọṛ
Milḽ'ạṛḍ Fḭll'mọ̆rẹ
Frănk'lĭn Pịerçẹ
Jāmẹṣ Būeḫ ăn'an
Ā'bra ham Lĭn'cọḫn
Ăn'drew Jŏḫn'sŏn
U lȳs'sēṣ Ṣ. Grănt
Rŭth'er fŏrd Ḇ. Hāyẹ̆ṣ
Jāmẹṣ Ạ. Gär'fïĕld
Chĕs'ter Ạ. Är'thur
Grō'ver Clēvẹ'land

Bĕn'ja mĭn Hăr'ri sŏn
Grover Cleveland.

www.ingramcontent.com/pod-product-compliance
Lightning Source LLC
Chambersburg PA
CBHW021917180426
43199CB00032B/418